REDISCOVERING

REDISCOVERING

Herbert Douglass

REVIEW AND HERALD® PUBLISHING ASSOCIATION
HAGERSTOWN, MD 21740

This book was
Edited by Raymond H. Woolsey
Cover illustration by Helcio Deslandes
Type set: 11/12 Times

PRINTED IN U.S.A.

96 95 94   10 9 8 7 6 5 4 3 2 1

R&H Cataloging Service
Douglass, Herbert E.
    Rediscovering joy.

    1. Bible.   N.T.   Philippians.   2. Bible.
N.T.   Colossians.   3. Joy and sorrow.
I. Title.

                227

ISBN 0-8280-0854-X

Contents

The Twilight of Joy

1

"Our recent studies show evidence of startling cultural changes . . . that penetrate to the core of American life—into the private spaces of our inner lives, the semipublic space of our lives within the family, at work, in school, in church, in the neighborhood, and into the public space of our lives as citizens. . . . Younger Americans are growing ever more fretful, anxious, off balance, and goalless. . . . Each year for the past several years the number of young Americáns who lack clearly defined goals and feel utterly aimless about their lives has increased" (Daniel Yankelovich, *New Rules: Searching for Self-Fulfillment in a World Turned Upside Down* [New York: Random House, 1981], pp. xiii-xiv).

MORE than interesting. As I write, across America graduates and invited speakers are singing in the minor key. And they seem to be reading off the same page and feeling the same way. Three observations:

At nearby Colfax High School the valedictorian pointedly reminded his peers and their many guests that their next step was into a "future of grim uncertainty" (Auburn *Journal,* June 13, 1993).

On the other side of the continent, the student body president at Gordon College, Wenham, Massachusetts, reflected: "From my view in the graduation line, things look disheartening. Gangs carve out city blocks for themselves. Lakes and rivers spit up gobs of trash and toxins. The holy priest is no longer wholly trusted, and society is fragmented by moral and cultural relativity. . . .

"Critiques of today's college students portray us as self-centered hedonists, and there is a lot of truth in that. But why shouldn't we grab all the gusto we can? Practically every message we have received, from childhood on, has been delivered in splashy, sexy, sensuous overtones. In psychological terms, the generation at the helm of the economy provided the stimulus; we are just providing the response. . . . Our generation looks at a bleak landscape" (*Christianity Today,* May 17, 1993, p. 21).

A 1992 graduate of Adelphi University commented: "In addition to being delighted, most new graduates also feel anxious and ambivalent. The immediate future looks dim. Thousands face unemployment; thousands more will face *under*employment.

"That is, due to the lack of available and appropriate career opportunities, many will be forced to take low-paying jobs in fields unrelated to those for which they are prepared. . . .

"Graduates of the nineties face a harsh reality: As far as career preparation is concerned, the money, time, and energy invested in their 'higher' education may well have been wasted" (*USA Today,* June 24, 1993).

This kind of language, echoing throughout America and the world generally, is a sea change compared to graduates even a generation ago. Since my high school graduation in 1944, the United States has gone through the horrific end to World War II, stopped Communism's sprawl in Korea at great price, and endured a most controversial bloodletting in Vietnam. We paid dearly for the 40 years of uncertainty called the cold war and experienced a period of scientific and technological advance that surpassed all previous history combined.

But through it all we heard and saw the zing of enthusiasm, the eagerness of young and old to seek one's dream—we were convinced that all we needed was a chance to work hard at whatever was available and to prove ourselves.

No more. Not for a decade or two. That ring of joyful anticipation has well-nigh vanished in Western countries—even though the rest of the world still comes to our shores seeking a better life. Paradoxically, the present generation, from the viewpoint of physical comfort, material convenience, and medical achievement, has never had it so good.

What's going on?

In James Patterson and Peter Kim's shocking yet credible blockbuster *The Day America Told the Truth,* we read: "As we entered the 1990s, it became suddenly and urgently clear that a tumultuous change was occurring in America and the rest of the world around us. On every front—love, marriage, and the family;

religion, politics, and the community; work, leisure, and our global position—the ground beneath our feet began shifting. Yesterday's verities had vanished. Unpredictability and chaos became the norm" (New York: Prentice Hall Press, 1991, p. 3).

And we wonder where joy has gone! Let's take a look at what scares today's graduates. What has happened in one generation or two to change so radically a young person's view of tomorrow?

If anyone has any doubts regarding the plate-tectonic shift during the past 30 years in the way people think about right and wrong, about responsibility and self-interest, about God, and about whatever else truly matters—read on. What follows is only a quick sampling of many well-respected observers:

"Three broad but sharply different styles . . . presently characterize the population of the United States. I call them the cultural left, the cultural middle, and the cultural right. The cultural left is made up largely of inner-directed, self-fulfilled baby boomers who are now [as of 1993] in their 20s, 30s, and 40s. Their lifestyle is a radical departure from that of all previous generations in the United States. . . .

"The cultural middle is constituted of those successful business and professional people who are career-oriented and seek to make it to the top. They are fulfillers of the American dream and live out—or strive to—the established values of the dominant culture. . . .

"The cultural right, the largest lifestyle group of the three, . . . are self-denying local people who hold tenaciously to traditional values and conventional morality. Their lifestyle is even more distant from the cultural left, which most do not understand and which many vigorously oppose. . . .

"It is important to understand that in using a left, middle, and right spectrum, I am not talking about political positions, but about lifestyles. While the cultural left is politically the most liberal of the group, the parallel ends there. . . . One can be culturally left and politically right, or vice versa" (*U.S. Lifestyles and Mainline Churches*, p. 4).

Writing in the midst of this generational transition (1979), Christopher Lasch warned about America's social life "becoming more warlike and barbaric" and the "collapse of personal life." He described with withering pen the decadence of social and cultural pursuits, the exhaustion of will. He put a modern touch on the term *narcissism* (love of one's own interests): "The concept of narcissism provides us . . . with a way of understanding the psychological impact of recent social changes. . . . It yields a tolerably accurate portrait of the 'liberated' personality of our time, with his charm, his pseudoawareness of his own condition, his promiscuous pansexuality, . . . his protective shallowness, his avoidance dependence, his inability to mourn, his dread of old age and death."

Looking at the national scene, he sees "a way of life that is dying—the pursuit of happiness to the dead end of a narcissistic preoccupation with the self, . . . a cultural revolution that reproduces the worst features of the collapsing civilization it claims to criticize" (*The Culture of Narcissism: American Life in an Age of Diminishing Expectations*, pp. 30, 50).

Robert E. Webber wrote in 1982: "Something has happened to America in the last two decades. No matter whom you talk to—ministers, teachers, doctors, lawyers, housewives, blue-collar or white-collar workers—most seem to agree a change has taken place, and it's not a welcomed change.

"'It's a permissive society,' a mother of three children said pensively. 'I don't like the temptations children have to face—it's a tough world in which to grow up.' 'Yes,' a young couple echo the thought. 'We're not sure we want to bring children into this society.'

"What is it that has made our society change in the last two decades? Why do many people feel uneasy about the future? What is the cause of the upsurge in free sex, abortion, incest, pornography, the threat of nuclear war, government control, invasion of privacy, distortion of the news, inflation, and unemployment?" (*Secular Humanism: Threat and Challenge*, p. 9).

No wonder our modern youth, and their parents and grandparents, find difficulty speaking to each other, regardless of their love for one another. No wonder so many find so little to hang their hopes on today—if all they saw is the horizontal picture!

Without the vertical dimension, truly no one has reason to look at tomorrow with any joy!

Let's take a look at the world as modern youth and their parents see it!

Think of us Californians—never mind what's happening elsewhere! Almost any newspaper will reflect the plight of the editor of our local Auburn *Journal,* responding to a reader who moaned, "I hope we don't have to see front pages with so much unpleasantness": "She was reacting to the May 4 *Journal* front page that included: a photo and story about the discovery of a knife that may have been used in an attempted sexual abduction; a story on the sentencing phase for a child molester-adult abuser; another on still another child molester being found guilty; and finally, rounding out the local part of page l, a story about an investigation linking a Rocklin rapist with similar crimes elsewhere.

"And if that wasn't enough, on the back page, where the stories continued, was a story about a conviction in a rape-murder. We couldn't agree more with the caller. This did amount to a massive dose of awful news—to call it 'unpleasantness' is a euphemistic kindness.

"But what's a paper to do? . . . Unfortunately those things happened. . . . As ugly as they were, our readers needed to know. Not one of these stories was from New York or L.A. They were local. . . .

"We didn't go out of our way to put out the sensational page in question. It was the news of the day" (May 23, 1993).

But on that same day were stories about the depleting of the water quality of the Sacramento-San Joaquin River Delta, erosion of the ozone layer, carbon monoxide from vehicle and industrial emissions, landfills, and radioactive radon gas emerging from soils beneath schools.

A few days before, a thoughtful columnist in the Sacramento *Bee* reflected on the current dilemma of California: "Unfortunately, the social and economic condition one finds in California these days stand in stark contrast to its picture postcard landscape. The economy remains mired in the worst recession in a half-century, crime and racial tensions plague California cities, and the elaborate infrastructure of first-class public services and facilities is decaying rapidly.

"Most alarmingly, we Californians seem to have lost our can-do spirit, our belief that all things are possible, that has always been the state's most valuable asset. This newly minted pessimism is reflected in the growing legions of Californians who are packing up and moving out" (May 2, 1993).

I have a strong suspicion that most of what drowns joy in California is well understood across the "fruited plains." In some places, especially, the closing of defense bases is a monstrous, numbing economic and social disaster that won't go away for decades. The downsizing of huge industrial complexes (many of which prided themselves in never laying off their workers, such as IBM, Proctor and Gamble, etc.) has clearly devastated hundreds of thousands of family groups—as well as having a ripple effect throughout the economy.

"For the first time on record, white-collar workers have surpassed blue-collar workers in the nation's unemployment lines. . . . 'We don't have an answer for these people [says a Columbia University economics professor in her new book *Declining Fortunes*], . . . if credentials, skills, and education can't protect you, then there is no recipe for security in the American job market'" (*U.S. News & World Report*, June 28, 1993, pp. 43, 44).

Let's look at ourselves from another direction: For all Americans, as well as other nations that have enjoyed immense prosperity in the twentieth century, the problem of national debt and deficit spending has become front-page agony. Financial letters, TV commentators, newspaper columnists, and living room "experts" seem to be simplifying the economic babble into such questions as: How can vastly higher taxes create prosperity? Where has any country in history taxed itself into a healthier economy? How can government spending do anything other than dissipate capital and reduce the will to invest and experiment, which would create more jobs?

Even contemplating those questions and observing a benumbing national drift only deepens the twilight of joy. Witness the editorial in *U.S. News & World Report,* May 17, 1993:

"What's going on here? What appears to be happening is that the historic parallel between increasing output and job creation may now be fractured and that this may make a chimera of full employment in a free society, that we may be in some kind of permanent jobs recession."

Let's turn the page in any weekly newsmagazine or Sunday paper. Look at the world hunger equation, which involves "economics and politics as much as it does science. . . . Most of the world's nearly 1 billion hungry today are starving not because of a food shortage but because of political turmoil or shortages of money. Even if hard work and massive agricultural investment can eke out enough food for 10 billion, a crucial question remains: Will the world's hungry have the money to afford it, or the political stability to ensure its efficient delivery" (*U.S. News & World Report*, Feb. 8, 1993, p. 55)? No joy in those bleak, wide-eyed bloated bellies of bewildering children!

Recent graduates are not alone in their dismal, sinking feeling about the future. The driving pull of joy evaporates *even before our young leave elementary school.* In a recent *Weekly Reader* survey of 60,000 U.S. students, we learned that "fewer youngsters today feel they have control over their lives. . . . This year's students in grades 4, 5, and 6 are less likely to think their own choices will determine their futures. . . . In 1989, 81 percent of those in grades 4-6 felt they would determine their futures. Now only 69 percent feel that way. . . . It suggests the need to reinforce students' belief in themselves, in school, and at home" (*USA Today*, June 2, 1993).

Underlying everything we have noted so far are those basic observations noted earlier regarding the astonishing cultural and social shifts of the past 30 years. Compare 1960 and 1994 in terms of AIDS; "free love" (is it ever really free?); the enormous rise in the number of divorces; drug- and violence-ridden schools, with their free condoms; single-parent families; regulated attempts to guarantee equal living standards at the expense of individual incentive; live-in partners; outing of bisexuals, gays, and lesbians; and on the list goes.

In *The Day America Told the Truth* we read the results of the shift in the basic moral guidelines that prevailed in the United States until 30 years ago. Following are some "major revelations" their research discovered:

"At this time, America has no leaders and, especially, no moral leadership. Americans believe . . . that our current political, religious, and business leaders have failed us miserably and completely. . . .

"Americans are making up their own rules, their own laws. In effect, we're all making up our own moral codes. Only 13 percent of us believe in all of the Ten Commandments. Forty percent of us believe in five of the Ten Commandments. We choose which laws of God we believe in. There is absolutely no moral consensus in this country as there was in the 1950s, when all our institutions commanded more respect. Today, there is very little respect for the law—for any kind of law. . . .

"Young American males are our biggest national tragedy. Males between the ages of 18 and 25 are the real cause of our crime problem. They are responsible for most child abuse. They are a violent, untrustworthy, and undependable group. At one time, our young men were disciplined in the military before entering the general population, but no more. . . .

"The official crime statistics in the United States are off by more than 600 percent. The recorded statistics are far too low. The amount of actual crime in the country is staggering. . . .

"Lying has become an integral part of the American culture, a trait of the American character. We lie and don't even think about it. We lie for no reason. The writer Vance Bourjaily once said, 'Like most men, I tell a hundred lies a day.' That's about right. And the people we lie to most are those closest to us. . . .

"Community, the hometown as we have long cherished it, no longer exists. There are virtually no hometowns anymore. More important, there is no meaningful sense of community. Most Americans do not participate in any community action whatsoever. . . .

"One in seven Americans has been sexually abused as a child—and one in six Americans has been physically abused as a child. . . .

"The ideal of childhood is ended. A startling percentage of American children lose their virginity before the age of 13. They're losing their childhood, all of their innocence, in other ways as well. . . .

"A letdown in moral values is now considered the number one problem facing our country. Eighty percent of us believe that morals and ethics should be taught in our schools again" (pp. 5-8).

Some picture of the twilight of joy!

But a counterculture is aborning. Crass materialism or instant self-gratification lived to the brim does not seem to satisfy most people for long. That fact accounts for the astounding rise of that enormously inclusive term the New Age movement. Here indeed is the modern search for the spiritual, for "meaning," propelled by the void in a culture that has rejected its traditional moral moorings. For most in this quest, it is an honest search for personal meaning and a sense of future. The pity is that so much of the longing, even much of the terminology, is biblically appropriate. But its solutions are 180 degrees alien to the revealed truths of the Holy Scriptures. More about this in chapter 10.

We have surveyed, ever so quickly, the reasons behind the "twilight of joy" that is so prevailing, so suffocating, throughout all age groups and economic strata in every land on earth.

Now the relevancy of this chapter to the purpose of this book (if I had stated it earlier I may have turned off some of my readers): All of us, Seventh-day Adventists included, are living in the same cultural and societal ocean. Changes in attitudes of responsibility toward historic and biblical norms within Adventist ranks are matters to be reviewed. Else we will discover ourselves thinking and doing whatever may be the "in thing" to do. After all, "everybody is doing it!"

Pause for a moment and reflect. Form a picture of Seventh-day Adventist beliefs and practices of 30-40 years ago and note: statistics are abundant that live-in partners, use of alcoholic beverages, single-parent families, the public declaration of gays and lesbians of their lifestyle, Sabbath-as-holiday rather than Sabbath-as-holy day, AIDS, divorce, child abuse, lying, teenage sex, etc., have become astonishing features in the lives of many church members. The above brief summary cannot be challenged, only regretted.

How come? Of all people, how could it be that some Seventh-day Adventists would come to that time when biblical principles would be preempted by the cultural principles of their day—"If it feels right, do it!" "Don't deny your deepest feelings—your inner self; your life potential may be at stake!" "Rules are made by the powerful [or the authoritarian figure in your life] to restrict [or control] the weak." "Everybody is entitled to whatever anyone else has—those are our rights!" "The Bible—and other traditional authorities—are really the product of their author's culture and must be reevaluated for their application in our day." (All these comments are direct quotes I have heard.)

I am writing this book to speak to all of us immersed in the sea change of the past 30 years, myself included. I want to be more aware of one of the basic laws of life—the law of cause and effect (Gal. 6:7). We all sooner or later will eat at the banquet of personal choices. Biblical principles are not a matter for us to "take or leave," depending upon our personal opinions at the moment.

In our focus on Philippians and Colossians, we will listen to Paul speak directly to the paradox of our times—that the more we focus on self (its passions and its "rights"), the more perplexed and unsure we become. The more we seek for a lifestyle liberated from traditional restraints, the less we find reasons for joy. Joy goes from twilight to eclipse—even for Seventh-day Adventists.

We can't escape the ocean in which we all swim. But we can determine how much of the ocean will get inside of us.

For all of us, the event of all ages is at hand. The twilight of joy will soon become the blackest of midnight for too many. The dawn of hope, the thrill of reality, the ring of truth, awaits all those who respond to the many reasons for joy that we will discuss in the next chapter.

Rediscovering Adventist Joy

2

"But let all those rejoice who put their trust in You; Let them ever shout for joy, because You defend them; Let those also who love Your name be joyful in You" (Ps. 5:11, NKJV).

IN THIS chapter I will focus on how Christians in general, and Adventists in particular, may break out of the self-defeating malaise called the twilight of joy so pervasive in the latter part of the twentieth century. This will be done in three steps: (1) we will quickly note that joy is a deeper experience than happiness or cheeriness; (2) we will discover that joy is built on facts (reasons) that have been tested in the crucible of life's experiences—facts that have been revealed by the Rock on which joy builds; and (3) we will investigate some of the factors that distinguish Christians who not only have joy but who carry the responsibility to share those reasons—and their joy—with others.

As we will discuss further in later chapters, joy transcends the circumstances of the present. Joy is not the same as happiness or gladness or cheeriness. Happiness is too often a matter of instant gratification—a new car, a dream vacation, or the pleasures of addictive drugs.

Many, for the sake of good manners or to be responsible when others aren't, brighten their homes or churches or workplaces with big smiles and kind words. But many cheery faces hide the gloom of disappointment, even despair—a heart void of joy.

Joy, however, is a deeper experience—far deeper than sensual satisfaction and material symbols of "success," beyond good manners and a courageous "upper lip." Joy sings amid pain, faces up to crumbling dreams, and helps us endure when the future is most uncertain.

I have never been more convinced—after decades of studying the most revered philosophers and theologians, after reviewing the options that spread themselves before us like a Sunday brunch at the Hyatt House—that the secret of joy rests in the words of Jesus: *"These things I have spoken to you, that My joy may remain in you, and that your joy may be full"* (John 15:11, NKJV).

Your joy and mine will deepen and become more empowering to the extent that we know "these things" that God has "spoken to" us through His many ways, beginning with Holy Scripture. *These are the facts, or reasons, that provide the foundation for joy.*

To know how God feels about you and me personally, to know how He wants us to think about the four most talked-about topics—the future; quality living; human dignity in a very divided, hostile world; and the meaning of human existence and life after death—is to know the rock of assurance, the peace under stress, and the joy that transcends every human predicament. There is no other way! No other kind of joy!

This kind of joy invigorated Paul, who was soon to be beheaded for his candid, fearless, public promotion of his Carpenter-Lord—who had Himself, a few years earlier, "for the joy that was set before him endured the cross" (Heb. 12:2).

Fellow apostle James also knew from experience what he wrote for the encouragement of others. Like him, the early believers were hounded and cut down for their simple proclamation of the gospel. Listen to him sing to his friends: "Count it all joy, my brethren, when you meet various trials, for you know that the testing of your faith produces steadfastness [literally, "endurance"—see Rev. 14:12]" (James 1:2).

Both Jesus and James knew the facts, the truth about life and death, according to the "these things" that God had "spoken to" them. Their steadfastness depended on faith—and faith created the reasons for joy. In later chapters we will discuss what *faith*, a word that has caused most of the theological problems and divisions within Christianity, means in the New Testament. But for now let us recognize that the knowledge faith possesses builds a personal relationship with God. Further, the reasons that structured our Lord's and James's faith experience are the same reasons that form the bedrock of Christian joy—especially Adventist joy in the unique responsibility resting on them. These reasons always have and always will be the mountain spring from which Adventist joy will flow until the end of time.

For one to cast about for a different foundation or a different fountain, or to attempt to "revise" Adventist history, invites only uncertainty, confusion, and ultimately, despair. Yes, casting about for new building blocks that mute the distinctiveness of the Adventist message will seem exhilarating. There will be days, perhaps years, of a strange, new sense of liberation, a sense of freedom without restraints—but the end is not joy. Ask Eve.

What are some of those reasons that Christians, and Adventists in particular, should live with profound joy?

For instance, why is it that Seventh-day Adventists have seemed to be one step ahead through the years when it has come to the dangers of smoking and high-cholesterol diets or the necessity of exercise?

Or why is it that whenever people worry about war in the Middle East, or even World War III, or the state of Israel in last-day prophecy, Adventists aren't in a panic? Why?

Some of our older members know how it used to be. For many years Seventh-day Adventists were lonely voices crying in a scoffing wilderness. From town to town they preached from their tents or rented halls a strange message: 1. The end of the world is at hand! 2. Tobacco, caffeine products, tea, alcoholic beverages, and many other generally accepted habits of diet, such as animal products, are detrimental to health! 3. Cities have unique, built-in liabilities that directly affect human well-being—more so as time passes. 4. The world's religious and economic leaders will move relentlessly toward world unity! 5. The papal system will assume an ever increasing importance in world affairs! And on the strange message went, as well as the ridicule.

But no more. Adventists are no longer lonely or appear strange. For instance, what have people been talking about in the past 30 years? The list is easy—check out the covers of *Time,*

Newsweek, or *U.S. News & World Report*: the uncertain future in a rapidly changing international reconfiguration; the quality of life in a suddenly polluted world; human dignity amid the Holocaust, difficulties in Cambodia, the dismemberment of Yugoslavia, as well as ethnic hostilities on every continent; personal meaning to human existence and life after death as reflected in the phenomenal rise of New Age channeling, reincarnation, and the human potential movement—to name a few prominent topics.

Obviously, these are Adventist subjects. But those who have been speaking the loudest on these subjects are not the Adventists, unfortunately. Adventists have not authored the runaway best-sellers on these subjects, such as Hal Lindsey's *The Late Great Planet Earth.* Nor have they sponsored those ubiquitous bumper stickers such as "Guess Who's Coming Again," "If You Love Jesus, Honk Twice," and "In Case of Rapture, This Car Will Be Unmanned."

Without question, people, young and old, are reading and talking about the future and health and the environment and self-fulfillment and city problems and "the new world order," etc.—more than they ever have since the 1840s. What a day to focus on God's solutions to all these problems and concerns!

But strange as it may seem, for some Adventists the distinctive Adventist position or solution to these contemporary concerns have lately been cause for embarrassment.

Thus, a plea to my heart and yours: To retain or recover Adventist joy is to discover anew the distinctiveness of basic Adventism. Let's now take a quick look at how basic Adventist thought looks at the previously mentioned "big" topics of our day.

What About the Future?

In general, people approach this subject in one of two ways—pessimistically or optimistically. The pessimists, for example, point to the population explosion worldwide; to world hunger that simply doesn't go away, no matter how much money is thrown at it; to the ghastly tentacles of the world drug menace—and say, in words that far outshout any Adventist warning:

"Unless we radically change our present pattern of living, no one will be around on this planet 100 years from now!" Or even 50 years, many say!

They cite the proliferation of nuclear weapons among many nations, some not known for stability. They record data on ozone breakdown, the greenhouse time bomb, the depletion of clean and available water worldwide, the staggering implications of world garbage, the smog suffocating many of the largest cities of the world—the list doesn't seem to stop.

But optimists look at the same world and come up smiling. They point to the astounding record of scientific and technological discoveries and breakthroughs that have dazzled and calmed us—just in the past 25 years! Take medical science, for example. Smallpox, diphtheria, polio, and cholera are now, for all practical purposes, wiped out as human problems. The eventual triumph of the laboratory over cancer, muscular sclerosis, cerebral palsy, brain disorders, and other physical and emotional nightmares is a reasonable expectation. In addition, genetic engineering for medical purposes is a phenomenal reason for optimism!

New sources of food through aquaculture (the raising of food where water is plentiful) and the wonders of biotechnology are here now. Tremendous increases in land production because of genetic improvements in seed strains is no longer fantasy. Ceramic engines, superconductors, new sources of energy, computerized marvels that continue to change how we think about communication, transportation—and even how we think about thinking—are just a few of the reasons why optimists discount the fears of the pessimists.

To make life even less stressful, think of the baby banks where prospective parents may order tiny, frozen embryos, guaranteed free from genetic defects and cataloged by color of hair and eyes, sex, size, IQ, etc. And accessible at the corner drugstore within the foreseeable future. You can now understand the dilemma facing some bystanders when they saw two men carrying signs. One sign read: "The world is about to end!" The second man's sign said: "The world will never end!" One of the bystanders said to the other, "One's a pessimist, and the other is an optimist. But I am not sure which is which!"

But for Adventists, the future will be much different than any other group in the earth sees it. The pessimists are wrong—the future is not hopeless. The world will not end in either a whimper or a bang. World nuclear powers will not incinerate the earth; we will not drown or be suffocated in our own garbage or foul air, nor will we shrivel up in mass starvation.

And the optimists are wrong—the future is not in the hands of ingenious men and women who up to now have always come up with nifty, wonderful, and lifesaving solutions. Technology will not cure, for example, the self-interest of relatives, neighbors, or nations. The rising tide of moral garbage will mock the rising standards of living now evident just about anywhere one goes on earth.

And yet the greatest threat to the spiritual eyesight of most men and women everywhere is precisely right here in the contagious spirit of optimism, regardless of what source it springs from—whether from scientific breakthroughs or from New Age razzmatazz.

The subtle breezes of optimism ("Everything's all right so far!") finally choked those who laughed at Noah. Our Lord kindly made it clear, "As were the days of Noah, so will be the coming of the Son of man" (Matt. 24:37).

Satan, the great deceiver, will do all he can to distract men and women regarding the future. Obviously, that's his business—and he is very good at what he does! But the Adventist mission is to tell the truth about the future—that our hope is in the visible, physical return of the crucified Carpenter, now serving as our heavenly High Priest. Not in reincarnation or a secret rapture or a millennial second chance or a purgatory transition or cryonics—no, not even in an immediate flight to heaven at death.

The truth about the future is that our Best Friend will step in as promised, on behalf of people who have become comfortable with His way of life. Not in a future to be feared, nor a nirvana of desires fulfilled, but in a renewed earth "wherein dwelleth righteousness." Neighborhoods in which people no longer hurt or destroy, a new world order for people who have chosen to set their neural pathways so that they will habitually love others and follow truth wherever it leads them, life without end.

Later in this book we will let Paul speak to us about the kind of people who will be safe to save in that "land of the beautiful forever."

Phenomenal Interest in the Quality of Life

No weekly newsmagazine, no daily paper, can be picked up that does not have at least one article on our worldwide urgency to protect endangered species, rain forests, and natural habitats. Or the dreadful consequences of carbon monoxide in crowded cities. The list seems endless. The dangers are real.

But even more phenomenal is our remarkable concern for knowledge relating to diet, health in general, and the prevention of disease. Physical-fitness programs, health spas, and health-food stores have sprung up around the world like desert flowers after a spring rain. Soaps are pulled off supermarket shelves—too much phosphate; atomic power stations are closed down or blocked in planning; oil-drilling leases are locked up in courts for years; factories are closed down and pesticides legislated off the market—all in the interest of quality of life.

Here again, Adventists can tell the truth about the quality of life for which men and women were created to enjoy. Clearly it must be said, and often: men and women do have a responsibility for their environment—the air we breathe, the water we drink, the birds and animals that keep life fascinating. Christian commitment does not relieve anyone from this stewardship (Gen. 1:26-30). Waste, filth, and the destruction of ecosystems (whether it begins in our closets and under our beds, or backyards, neighborhoods, cities, and nations) are the works of shortsighted or lazy or greedy men and women who do not understand their responsibility as entrusted stewards.

But let's make all this even more personal. The quality of life that we enjoy will depend directly upon the way we eat, exercise, and utilize the many components of health, such as copious water, regular sunlight, fresh air, and ample sleep. In addition, we must discipline ourselves to select the best options available and to trust joyfully in the wisdom and guidance offered to us by our Creator-Friend.

The truth about quality living is that a simple compliance to basic health laws (which are no longer dark secrets) forms the only kind of environment wherein peace of mind and energy to be vigorous, positive, gracious, and constructive can flourish.

From where I see it, Seventh-day Adventists have been putting the package together for more than a century, long before conventional medical wisdom saw the first gleams of our headlights. We can tell the world, now more eager for information regarding quality living, that healthful living is more than a concern for longevity, or Slenderella figures, or beach-boy physiques, or even the best way to avoid disease.

The point of healthful living is that the laws of health have much to do with a person's mental well-being and the development of character. Any goal less than that is to use the modern emphasis on health for mere selfish, self-centered purposes.

We are overwhelmed these days with laboratory research supporting the profound relationship between the physical, the mental, and the spiritual. Such data validate the wisdom of statements written more than a century ago, such as: "The body is the only medium through which the mind and the soul are developed for the upbuilding of character" (*Counsels on Diets and Foods,* p. 73). "The brain nerves which communicate with the entire system are the only medium through which Heaven can communicate to man and affect his inmost life" (*Testimonies,* vol. 2, p. 347).

Basic Adventism has placed a towering emphasis on healthful living primarily because clear, discerning minds can best appreciate the truths about God (Heb. 5:14). Healthy bodies and minds are more apt to be patient and enthusiastic in relating to others. Healthy minds focused on truth are more apt to be eager to share those truths with others rather than sit at home exhausted and weary for lack of exercise and proper nutrition (Rom. 12:1, 2).

In a certain sense, our regard for the quality of life will determine our fitness to live forever. Such thoughts are stuff of which joy is made.

Worldwide Hunger for Human Dignity

The political configuration of the 184 nations that belong to the United Nations ranges from totalitarian dictatorships on one hand to unbridled charades of democracy on the other. Even within those countries that are well known for their diligence in providing equal opportunity for all their citizens, various groups exist that feel they are denied full expression of individual rights, for either religious or ethnic or gender reasons.

Questions exist such as: How much inconvenience should the minority expect the majority to put up with? Is each person's opinion as valid or as useful as anyone else's? Who gives in first—the majority or the minority?

These age-old questions have never been more crucial, more ominous, than today. They will become increasingly more severe and pervasive in every land as the end of time draws nearer.

We have only to recall the events of the past five years for fresh examples of that worldwide hunger for human freedom and individual dignity. Think of that young Chinese student, implausibly resolute, who held up a long line of lumbering tanks in Beijing's Tiananmen Square, shouting: "Why are you here?" at the momentarily silent steel monster. That episode, pictured on the cover of *Time*, June 19, 1989, freezes the age-old human dilemma on a sin-laden planet—a drama that will become increasingly relevant as the future gallops toward us.

But the problem of individual rights versus the power of government and the responsibility of the majority has tantalized philosophers since Plato's *Republic*. On what basis, by what philosophical theory, do we answer these basic questions that determine how anyone thinks about how much value or respect is due anyone? If we believe that humanity slowly oozed up from primeval mud, simply the modern product of the survival of the fittest—who decides, and on what basis, the worth of the individual? Without understanding why each person deserves dignity and respect, appeals to human dignity and individual "rights" soon degenerate into passing waves of sentimentalism and warm fuzzies.

Adventists, one of very few Christian groups yet existing, can tell the truth about the basis for human dignity: We were created

25

"in the image of God," to be the friendly Creator's counterparts! Not through some kind of God-inspired evolution—a century-old viewpoint into which most Christians today have capitulated—but *"by the word of the Lord. . . . For he spoke, and it came to be; he commanded, and it stood forth"* (Ps. 33:6-9; see also Gen. 1).

The reason that Adventists have not capitulated to the prevailing worldview does not rest only in the Genesis story (which so many count as interesting mythology) or in the Creation references here and there throughout the Bible. The bedrock authority that validates the Genesis story is carved in the Ten Commandments.

No one who truly accepts the enduring quality of the Ten Commandments can ever become an evolutionist, not even a theistic evolutionist. Why? Because of the Sabbath commandment! How simple, how clear: *"For in six days, the Lord made heaven and earth, the sea, and all that is in them, and rested the seventh day; therefore the Lord blessed the sabbath day and hallowed it"* (Ex. 20:11).

Therefore, we were never created to be mere individuals whose inalienable rights were to be free "to do his own thing," to do it "my way," as the song goes. Adventists can tell the truth about the foundation for an individual's worth—men and women were created to be responsible beings (beings able to respond), not merely breathing, reasoning animals at liberty to follow instinct and sensual desire without bounds and moral consequences.

Because of humanity's high calling, the value set at their creation, Adventists look on every person, in every land, regardless of racial origin or gender, as a very important individual with great worth and with great possibilities regarding his or her future. Because of this supreme worth as God's counterparts (persons who can relate in friendship and love to the Person), Adventists have a heavy responsibility to make this good news clear: no man or woman is truly free who tries to be emancipated from his friendly Creator's counsel.

In Worcester, Massachusetts, in the heart of New England, stands the county courthouse. Atlantic Union College is nearby in South Lancaster, one of the loveliest towns on earth. Often in my college days, and then during 10 years of administration, I would frequently pass that granite building. Each time I read again, like a ritual for me, those words chiseled into the frieze above the pillars: "Obedience to law is liberty."

That is the Adventist answer to the free-wheeling individual "rights" groups that ebb and flow through the generations—often so selective, so symbolic, without substance: Genuine human dignity rests on the value our friendly Creator gave to us at Creation, and reaching our individual potential rests on how closely we listen to His advice.

How to Find Personal Meaning

The past 30 years have seen an astonishing, unabashed interest in "personal meaning," interchanges with "supernatural beings," "after-death" experiences, and Eastern religions. No longer is "spiritualism," or "spiritism," kept behind closed-curtain séances with their candles and dark shadows. (I remember vividly such experiences in a nearby residence when I was a boy.)

Today highly visible people in government and entertainment talk or write freely about their occult experiences. Channeling, reincarnation, and much of the human-potential movement have become front-page news, no longer restricted to wild stories in lurid papers such as the *National Enquirer.*

But let us not be blind or deaf. Most of those fascinated by the New Age movement seek truth and personal meaning as honestly as anyone reading these pages. So many are weary of the stereotyped platitudes of organized religion. They long for personal assurance and meaning in a world of group-think and materialistic substitutes for spiritual answers. They are tired of churches that are more interested in self-preservation than in sharing solutions that truly satisfy the deepest questions of the human heart. And many are disenchanted with Christian symbols without substance, with theological babble offering cheap grace, without a difference.

It seems to me that Seventh-day Adventists alone can speak clearly and convincingly about the modern cry for meaning, a meaning that includes a credible picture of life after death. The reason: Adventists accept the biblical teaching regarding the nature of man and the conditions on which eternal life is based. Whenever we get confused about such terms as the soul, about the biblical concept of the resurrection, and about the time of judgment, our confidence in humanity's existence after death becomes muddled and pure sentiment.

But clearness of thought about life after death is enhanced not only by the sheer force of Bible texts, but also by a self-authenticating fellowship with our friendly Lord and His Spirit. Adventists know that there is no joy or salvation in merely reciting biblical texts or agreeing with denominational doctrine; unless the voice of Jesus is heard speaking directly to the soul when the Bible is read, religion soon becomes a bore—or worse, a meaningless burden.

The truth about the future gets hazy, perhaps even unimportant—if one does not have a deep sense of relationship with our Lord. Everyone reading these words knows exactly what I mean. But in this relationship lies the answer to the question Who am I? Personal meaning—a lasting, deepening, unshakable conviction—comes when we seek the highest good for those around us, testing what that good should be by what God says the highest good is.

Personal meaning and self-fulfillment are not found by looking within, not found by testing truth by how anything "feels," but by listening to our friendly Lord, who once lived on the same basis as we must, 2,000 years ago in Palestine. He knows our temptations, our basic desires, our deepest hopes—and He alone can help us find inner strength to cope with life's surprises and demands. Nehemiah discovered this open secret through the toughest of times: "The joy of the Lord is your strength" (Neh. 8:10).

The Adventist Advantage

We have briefly discussed the major topics occupying the minds of people today—the future, the quality of life, the hunger for human dignity, and the pursuit of personal meaning extending to life after death.

These prime-time concerns have given Seventh-day Adventists a most favorable, most providential hour in which to state their distinctive message to a weary and waiting world.

Make no mistake about it—there is not the slightest reason to falter at this point; Adventists have the advantage and the responsibility. It is precisely this advantage that God expects Seventh-day Adventists to make plain to their loved ones and neighbors the world over.

They can speak out without the uneasy feeling that they may be riding only a temporary wave, or a sentimental fad that will be replaced by some other media-popularized interest. What Adventists have to say about the future, about the quality of life, about human freedom, about how to find personal meaning to life, has been *their distinctive message for over a century.* The validity of this unique, full-orbed message has never been more vindicated than today when these subjects are on everyone's lips.

In a very special way, because of the writings of Ellen White, Seventh-day Adventists have had the advantage. Dr. J. H. Kellogg, medical superintendent of the then world famous Battle Creek Sanitarium, was in his prime in 1895. Talking to young Dr. David Paulson, who was just finishing his medical training, Kellogg asked, "Do you know how it is that the Battle Creek Sanitarium is able to keep five years ahead of the medical profession?"

Young Paulson said modestly that he did not know. Then Dr. Kellogg explained, "When a new thing is brought out in the medical world, I know from my knowledge of the Spirit of Prophecy whether it belongs in our system or not.

"If it does, I instantly adopt it and advertise it while the rest of the doctors are slowly feeling their way, and when they finally adopt it, I have five years' start on them.

"On the other hand," he continued, "when the medical profession is swept off their feet by some new fad, if it does not fit the light we have received, I simply do not touch it. When the doctors finally discover their mistake, they wonder how come I did not get caught too" ("Critique of *Prophetess of Faith*" [White Estate, 1974]).

Dr. Kellogg was a world leader in his field because of the Adventist advantage. Precisely these advantages are what our friendly Lord expects Seventh-day Adventists to make plain to the world today.

Advantages do not exist merely to perpetuate themselves. They are "sent people"—sent to share some remarkable advantages to men and women. These advantages are Adventist reasons for Adventist joy.

But Adventist advantages are double-edged. Each advantage is a responsibility—a call to be useful and alert and ready and gracious and believable! God is waiting for such a people entrusted with these advantages to make creditable all this good news of His kingdom.

Adventist joy cannot be bottled up and stored away for some distant time of trouble. Joy, by definition, is an experience to be shared. In this sense, our friendly God needs us very much. You are as important to Jesus as He is important to you. Sharing these advantages are simply His plan for setting the universe straight as to right and wrong and their respective consequences.

Adventist joy is renewed or rediscovered when we keep clarifying the revealed truths about life's greatest concerns. Joy is self-authenticating—it provides its own evidence. That's our friendly Lord's promise: *"But now I am coming to thee; and these things I speak in the world, that they may have my joy fulfilled in themselves" (John 17:13).*

In the following chapters, as we let Paul speak to us through his letters to the Philippians and the Colossians, we will hear more clearly those reasons for joy that captured Paul's heart. And the reasons on which your joy will build. I promise!

Jesus Finishes
What He Starts

3

"I am sure that he who began a good work in you will bring it to completion" (Phil. 1:6).

SOUNDS easy, doesn't it! Can the good news be that good? Paul was so confident that his friendly Lord will finish what He starts that he could say shortly before his own execution: "I have fought the good fight, I have finished the race, I have kept the faith. Henceforth there is laid up for me the crown of righteousness, which the Lord, the righteous judge, will award to me on that Day, and not only to me but also to all who have loved his appearing" (2 Tim. 4:7, 8). You and I should also enjoy this confidence. Such confidence helps form the basis of Christian joy. Let's live that joy!

But how does this happen? Do we have any responsibility in helping our Lord finish what He starts? If so, we surely want to get it right! Let's think about it.

In the first chapters of the letters to the Philippians and to the Colossians, Paul defines what this "good work" is that Jesus brings to "completion":

"It is my prayer that your love may abound more and more, with knowledge and all discernment, so that you may approve what is excellent, and may be pure and blameless for the day of Christ, filled with the fruits of righteousness which come through Jesus Christ, to the glory and praise of God" (Phil. 1:9-11). "Of this you have heard before in the word of the truth, the gospel

31

which has come to you, as indeed in the whole world it is bearing fruit and growing. . . . We have not ceased to pray for you, asking that you may be filled with the knowledge of his will in all spiritual wisdom and understanding, to lead a life worthy of the Lord, fully pleasing to him, bearing fruit in every good work and increasing in the knowledge of God" (Col. 1:6-10).

Jesus said it earlier: "By this my Father is glorified, that you bear much fruit" (John 15:8).

Whatever else may be said, Paul and Jesus expect something significant to happen to us that not only pleases our heavenly Friend but also helps to vindicate His judgment before the universe. God has put Himself on record that He is able to produce the "fruits of righteousness" in once confirmed rebels. And He does this by planting the seeds of the truth—the gospel—in our minds so that gospel principles permeate our habits of thinking and doing. In fact, Paul told the Colossians that the goal of the gospel is to produce lives *"worthy of the Lord, fully pleasing to him."*

This expectation is awesome, almost beyond words. Just to contemplate what God has in mind for each of us is breathtaking. Almost too good to be true! Except that we are talking about the truth of the gospel! And our friendly Lord is very good about what He does!

Paul and Jesus chose their words carefully. Knowing that they were discussing matters of eternal importance, they wanted to be clearly understood. So they chose words and used analogies that would be as clearly understood by common fishermen and backyard gardeners as by the intellectual Greek or Roman in their day, and by college graduates in ours.

Comparing the kingdom of God, for example, to a fishing net or seed-sowing and harvest (Matt. 13; Mark 4; Luke 8) revealed our Lord's grasp of clear communicating principles: the hearer must "see" and "hear" clearly what the speaker or writer is trying to convey. Spiritual truths can be taught best when they are related to experiences that hearers know best.

That is why Paul and Jesus often used events associated with backyard gardens or the sweeping fields of grain to teach important truths about how God works out the plan of salvation in our lives. We call this emphasis on comparing the development of the Christian life with the growth of seed and its harvest the "harvest principle." The harvest principle is not a concept wrapped in a mystery and left for only trained theologians to understand. Because Jesus and Paul wanted to be very clear about the gospel, it was designed to be relevant and understandable.

So we ask, What does the harvest principle teach us about the plan of salvation?

First of all, for clues it points us to our gardens, our grapevines, and our apple trees. We all know the excitement of looking forward to plump, red tomatoes or juicy Mackintosh apples! See, you are already beginning to get the idea behind "the harvest principle."

Many of you know the feeling. Sometimes before the ground is really ready to plant we are in our gardens, working the compost into the warming soil. The inner excitement of "Here we go again!" compels us to join the robins as we line up our rows of early peas and carrots, waiting for the warmer soil before we plant our beans and tomatoes. The joy of the gardener or the wheat rancher!

But even though we truly enjoy the extra effort of planting the garden, and even the prospect of spending many pleasant weeks cultivating and weeding, all this satisfaction is not the reason we plant our seeds or trees. We plant because we expect a harvest!

However, when corn, tomatoes, beans, and wheat are planted, do we know the day when each crop will be ready for harvest? In a way, yes. Look at your favorite seed catalog. When we turn to the pages listing the variety of corn seeds available, each is described in detail and its growing season specified. Early corn should be ready in 68 days, other varieties in 72 or 78 days. And so we plan our gardens in advance, planting so that we will have corn ready for harvest throughout the summer, beginning with the sixty-eighth day.

But do we determine when our corn is ripe by merely crossing off the prescribed number of days on our kitchen calendar? Do we put the big pot on the stove, bring the water to boil, and then head for the garden to pick the corn because the seed catalog said that the corn is mature in 68 days? Wise gardeners don't!

No, part of the fun of growing corn is to watch the filling out of the ears. Then after looking around to see if anyone is looking (who hasn't?), we peel back the husk ever so slightly so that we can see whether the kernels are fully filled out. If not, we pat the green sheath firmly back around the ear and wait maybe another week before we look again. Right?

Was the seed catalog wrong when it stated categorically that the early corn would be ready in 68 days? Not at all! The catalog tells us when the harvest *should* be mature, when it *could* be picked—*if* all growing conditions have been favorable. But if the summer is abnormally hot or cold, too dry or too wet, or if the ground is undernourished, the time and the quality of the harvest could be directly affected. And so wise gardeners wait. We wait until the harvest is ripe, sometimes much later than we had first hoped because of the less-than-desirable conditions that thwarted their original schedule.

All that we seem to know about our gardens will help us understand two aspects about the gospel: (1) we learn how Jesus "grows" Christians, and (2) we learn why His return to this earth has been so long delayed.

Perhaps Jesus and Paul chose to compare God's work on the human heart and the timing of His return to a farmer's harvest because He knew that men and women everywhere would understand. Whether a farmer growing cotton along the Nile, or a wheat rancher in North Dakota, or an apple grower in Washington State, or high-rise condo owners in New York City with their balcony tomatoes—all understand, to some degree, the hopes and problems connected with harvesting their "crop."

Listen to Jesus compare both aspects of the harvest principle: "The kingdom of God is as if a man should scatter seed upon the ground, and should sleep and rise night and day, and the seed should sprout and grow, he knows not how. The earth produces of itself, first the blade, then the ear, then the full grain in the ear. But when the grain is ripe, at once he puts in the sickle, because the harvest has come" (Mark 4:26-29).

When Jesus was describing to John on Patmos how and when He would return to earth, He reemphasized the harvest principle.

Here lies the key to why we seem to be living during a delayed harvest in the twentieth century: "I looked, and lo, a white cloud, and seated on the cloud one like a son of man, with a golden crown on his head, and a sharp sickle in his hand. And another angel came out of the temple, calling with a loud voice to him who sat upon the cloud, 'Put in your sickle, and reap, for the hour to reap has come, for the harvest of the earth is fully ripe.' So he who sat upon the cloud swung his sickle on the earth, and the earth was reaped" (Rev. 14:14-16).

Our Lord's lesson is that the goals for our personal lives, the kingdom of God, and the field of grain are the same: to produce a harvest. Obviously, none of the three are ready to harvest unless the seed has matured. Even as the farmer must wait for his seed to mature, so Jesus will wait. A number of issues involved in the great controversy between good and evil must be resolved. He will wait until the gospel seed has produced a significant group of "fully ripe" Christians—a worldwide group that rightly reflects (thus giving a faithful witness to) the principles of His kingdom (Matt. 24:14).

Reflecting on the meaning of our Lord's parable about seed-time and harvest, a gifted writer observed: "The object of the husbandman in the sowing of the seed and the culture of the growing plant is the production of grain. . . . So the divine Husbandman looks for a harvest as the reward of His labor and sacrifice. Christ is seeking to reproduce Himself in the hearts of men; and He does this through those who believe in Him. The object of the Christian life is fruit bearing—the reproduction of Christ's character in the believer, that it may be reproduced in others" (*Christ's Object Lessons*, p. 67).

Could this quotation state the harvest principle any more clearly? Our Lord's purpose in bringing salvation to you and me is unambiguous. And the high goal set before the Christian could not be said more simply: the object of the gospel is to implant truth in the believer's "heart" for the purpose of a fully ripe harvest—a Christlike character.

But there is more to the biblically based harvest principle. Farmers and prophets have several things in common, the chief of which is that both engage in conditional prophecies: farmers know, for example, that the seed catalog promises that early corn *could* be ready in 68 days *if* . . . But the *if* is often beyond the farmer's control.

Similarly, our Lord is saying to us that the delay in the harvest of this world has not resulted from a change of mind on the part of the divine Husbander. As far as God is concerned, the harvest could have, and should have, ripened decades ago. We now live in the time of the delayed harvest. The fruit—persons who faithfully reflect the character of Jesus—has not yet reached the maturity that God looks for. And the divine Husbander has not, and will not, change the conditions on which the final harvest depends.

We should listen carefully to the following insight (1901) regarding the delayed Advent: "We may have to remain here in this world because of insubordination many more years, . . . but for Christ's sake, His people should not add sin to sin by charging God with the consequences of their own wrong course of action" (*Evangelism*, p. 696).

Unequivocally, as clearly as words can convey thought, Ellen White declared the sad yet challenging truth that the return of Jesus was already delayed in the 1880s. (In my earlier book *The End* you will find a list of 31 Ellen White references regarding the delayed Advent.)

Here in the 1990s our friendly Lord continues to wait until His church on earth catches on to their primary assignment and responsibility—to credibly preach "the gospel of the kingdom . . . throughout the whole world" (Matt. 24:14). Credible proclamation happens when gospel truth is fleshed out in the lives of its witnesses. Without a living demonstration of gospel principles, "the gospel of the kingdom" loses its credibility. Why should anyone listen to such preaching if it does not "work" in the lives of its advocates?

Many have been the words written emphasizing this dynamic union of life and word—the union of walk and talk: "We will glorify our Father in heaven in proportion as we purify and perfect our characters here. The greatest possible good we can do to our fellowmen is to overcome our own faults and improve our characters, making them as excellent and symmetrical as possible. Then our influence upon our fellowmen will be more effectual than even the pulpit labor of the most learned ministers without their seeking to improve the character and purify the life. Let your light so shine before men that they, in seeing your good works, may glorify our Father which is in heaven" (*Manuscript Releases*, book 9, p. 21).

"Excellent and symmetrical characters" have it all put together: the gospel seed is fully ripened—they are the kind of people who can be trusted no matter what the pressure, no matter how long. Such people live with joy day and night—because they sense their companionship with their heavenly Friend, regardless of earthly circumstances.

This is exactly what Paul was describing in the first chapter of Philippians: "So that you may approve what is excellent, and may be pure and blameless for the day of Christ, filled with the fruit of righteousness" (verse 10).

But fruit was meant to be harvested, remember? "When the grain is ripe, at once he puts in the sickle, because the harvest has come" (Mark 4:29). Those who work in hope for the Advent to come in their day can believe that our Lord will not wait one day past that moment when the decision is made by the last deciding person to join those "who keep the commandments of God and the faith of Jesus" (Rev. 14:12).

Yet Jesus must wait until each person in that last generation has had a fair opportunity to see the convincing evidence that His way is best. He must wait "with longing desire for the manifestation of Himself in His church. When the character of Christ shall be perfectly reproduced in His people, then He will come to claim them as His own. It is the privilege of every Christian not only to look for but to hasten the coming of our Lord Jesus Christ. . . . Were all who profess His name bearing fruit to His glory, how quickly the whole world would be sown with the seed of the gospel. Quickly the last great harvest would be ripened, and Christ would come to gather the precious grain" (*Christ's Object Lessons*, p. 69).

"Bearing fruit to His glory" has been God's purpose for men

and women since Eden. But glorifying God has become even more important as the seeds of sin have well-nigh eclipsed the truth about God and about the high destiny open to every human being. Sin has brought dishonor to God's name and has cast doubts on His character. (For further reading, see *Steps to Christ*, p. 11; *Education*, p. 154; *Patriarchs and Prophets*, p. 69.)

Questions such as the following have tested human minds for thousands of years: Is God not powerful enough to destroy sin, suffering, and death? Has He asked the impossible from His creation when He calls for their obedience while threatening them with hellfire for disobedience? Does His so-called mercy really deal with the sin problem?

To help answer these questions, Jesus came to this earth. Among many other reasons, His two chief purposes were to tell the truth about God and to show us how human beings can help Him deal with the sin problem. (We will discuss more about why Jesus came to earth and took human flesh in chapter 5.)

To further answer these questions, our heavenly Friend also turns to His people: "As thou didst send me into the world, so I have sent them into the world" (John 17:18).

What could Christians possibly do to help settle the sin problem? How could Christians help to remove the charges leveled against God and thus help to conclude the ever-so-long great controversy that Satan, the adversary, initiated in heaven (Rev. 12)?

What is the controversy all about? The central point of the great controversy between God and Satan, the first rebel, is whether God is truly loving, unselfish, just, wise, gracious, and worthy of His creation's admiration and trust. Satan convinced one third of the angels that God is not what He said He was. Astonishing, isn't it?

Who is winning? How would the world and the unfallen angels know if Satan was correct in his charges? Is it a matter of who shouts the loudest? How has God been revealing the truth about Himself and about the consequences of rebellion? Has His "good news" made any difference when His professed people are measured on the scale of unselfish love, fairness, and trustworthiness?

John witnessed that Jesus revealed the glory of God, "full of grace and truth" (John 1:14). During His 33 years, our Lord answered or uncovered Satan's lies regarding the true character of God. Further, our faithful Friend revealed what men and women could be like if they sought the same enabling power as He did daily (John 15:10; Rev. 3:21).

But Satan's reply (and often the reply of even many professed Christians) is that Jesus was, after all, different than all created beings: Jesus was God in human flesh, and of course, God could do what He wanted to do, the argument goes. Or, they say, because Jesus was born somewhat differently than other babies, He never really felt or understood the temptations, risks, and impediments that babies inherit when born into this world.

In chapter 5 we will discuss more about Christ's humanity—a subject that exceeds the length and depth and height of human thought. But pushing those limits in listening to revealed truth is our greatest challenge and the source of our greatest joy. Truly!

But for now let us let the harvest principle help us to understand how God's people will participate in clearing His name in the great controversy. For instance, when Jesus and Paul announced forgiveness and power to obey, how did all this "good news" begin to solve the sin problem on Planet Earth? How would a bystander know that all this information was more than mere symbolic talk? Was there a corresponding difference in those who "believed" the gospel?

Was it fair for Jesus to answer the question "What good deed must I do, to have eternal life?" with "If you would enter life, keep the commandments" (Matt. 19:16, 17)?

Did Paul place an impossible guilt trip on his readers when he wrote, "Be imitators of God. . . . Walk in love, as Christ loved" (Eph. 5:1, 2)? Or "Be pure and blameless for the day of Christ" (Phil. 1:10)? Or "Lead a life worthy of the Lord, fully pleasing to him, bearing fruit in every good work" (Col. 1:10)?

Or did Peter when he wrote, "As he who called you is holy, be holy yourselves in all your conduct" (1 Peter 1:15)?

Or John when he wrote, "He who says he abides in him ought to walk in the same way in which he [Jesus] walked" (1 John 2:6)?

The living answer to these questions is found in the confidence and encouragement of Paul's Prison Epistles (Ephesians, Philippians, and Colossians). Yes, God's faithful followers, once rebels, can become living evidence that God's power is in His promises. Their cheerful obedience brings glory to God—they prove the fairness of God's government, vindicate His besmirched character, and answer for all time to come regarding the deceit and unfairness of Satan's charges.

The linkage between Jesus bringing glory to the Father (John 17:18) and the similar assignment given to the church is reflected in this awesome statement: "The Saviour came to glorify the Father by the demonstration of His love; so the Spirit was to glorify Christ by revealing His grace to the world. The very image of God is to be reproduced in humanity. The honor of God, the honor of Christ, is involved in the perfection of the character of His people" (*The Desire of Ages*, p. 671).

During one of Israel's bleakest moments, God reminded His people through Ezekiel that He still was willing to work with and through them. Even during their miserable exile, the rest of the world would still get a true picture of His fairness and love for all human beings. Scattered as they were in Babylon and elsewhere, this tragedy depicted the fairness of God. He simply would not have His name profaned by those who bore it, nor would He allow it to appear to others as if He would do nothing about it: "I scattered them among the nations, and they were dispersed through the countries; in accordance with their conduct and their deeds I judged them. But when they came to the nations, wherever they came, they profaned my holy name, in that men said of them, 'These are the people of the Lord, and yet they had to go out of his land.' But I had concern for my holy name which the house of Israel caused to be profaned among the nations to which they came" (Eze. 36:19-21).

But hope was still there! Defeat, disgrace, despair—all consequences of personal and national foolishness, all there, but still there was hope! God was still willing to work with them. The future need not be a repeat of the past! Here's the promise: "I will vindicate the holiness of my great name, which has been profaned among the nations. . . . A new heart I will give you, and a new spirit I will put within you; and I will take out of your flesh the heart of stone and give you a heart of flesh. And I will put my spirit within you, and cause you to walk in my statutes and be careful to observe my ordinances. . . . Then you will remember your evil ways, and your deeds that were not good; and you will loathe yourselves for your iniquities and your abominable deeds. . . . Then the nations that are left round about you shall know that I, the Lord, have rebuilt the ruined places, and replanted that which was desolate; I, the Lord, have spoken, and I will do it" (verses 23-36).

Such was Paul's concern in his letters to the Philippians, the Colossians, and the Ephesians. For God's sake, Paul writes, the word of the truth should bear fruit *"to the glory and praise of God"* (Phil. 1:11). What could give friends of God more joy than to bring their heavenly Friend glory and praise?

God is glorified in persons who reflect His glory, who act like His sons and daughters. We say often that a father is generally recognized for what he is by the characteristics of faithful sons: "He is a chip off the old block," or "An apple doesn't fall far from the tree." Never more true, or more everlastingly important, than when we hear Jesus declare: "By this my Father is glorified, that you bear much fruit" (John 15:8)—the harvest principle.

Such is the responsibility resting on those who respond to God's last invitation of mercy in these last days. The first angel of Revelation 14 declares to all who will listen: "Fear God and give him glory, for the hour of his judgment has come" (verse 7). We must not miss the importance of this call to duty and joy: "To give glory to God is to reveal His character in our own, and thus make Him known" (*SDA Bible Commentary*, Ellen G. White Comments, vol. 7, p. 979).

Is this reality? Who has this capability to "glorify God"? That's the rub! How can rebels with a life record of selfishness and impurity ever expect to "reflect the image of Jesus fully" (*Early Writings*, p. 71)? Are these expectations suggesting the impossible? Is the harvest principle merely an ideal? Will God in reality work everything out in some other way? Does such language offer only gloom, discouragement, and despair? Hardly, as many joyful Christians have learned over the centuries!

In later chapters, especially chapter 10, we will let Paul tell us how God empowers His earthly friends to fulfill their potential as His sons and daughters. We will examine what it means to "glorify God—especially during these days when God's people have the privilege of proclaiming the messages of the three angels (Rev. 14).

In understanding our privileges and God's promises, we discover the rock-bottom support for lasting joy, regardless of circumstances. In our next chapter we will let Paul tell us how we set priorities so that the "growing" process keeps on God's schedule. What a joy to know that God has the plan for our lives—we don't have to figure it out by ourselves!

Philippians 1:12-30

Getting Our Priorities Straight

4

"For to me to live is Christ. . . . I know that I shall remain and continue with you all, for your progress and joy in the faith. . . . Only let your manner of life be worthy of the gospel of Christ. . . . For the sake of Christ you should not only believe in him but also suffer for his sake, engaged in the same conflict which you saw and now hear to be mine" (Phil. 1:21-30).

FAUST, a German magician in the early 1500s, amazed his audiences with spectacular tricks and far-fetched boasts. He claimed to be in league with the devil!

After his death, the character of Faust became a frequent component of plays, as well as the subject of many stories and poems—all focusing on what happens to a person who sells his soul to the devil in exchange for either magical powers or whatever else his heart desires. This exciting fulfillment of his highest wishes would last 24 years, after which the devil would drag Faust down to hell.

The Faustian theme has been captivating through the centuries because it plays out the universal dilemma that everyone faces sooner or later: Why does my life have so much disappointment and pain? What am I willing to pay for what I think will make me happy?

For many people reading these pages, the deal with the devil was struck years ago. The proverbial "24 years" has passed all too quickly! Perhaps in just one night! But read on. There's hope for you!

Jesus asked the same question: "What will it profit a man, if he gains the whole world and forfeits his life? Or what shall a man give in return for his life?" (Matt. 16:26).

Jesus Himself was offered the Faustian deal—the most important decision one can ever make! He showed us how to face the same compelling offer when the devil comes to us time and time again.

In Matthew 4 we watch Jesus entering the wilderness after His baptism "to be tempted by the devil" (verse 1). He faced the same entrancing temptations that all men and women must meet, not once, but often. Instead of going down the garden path, selling His soul for immediate gratification, He broke new paths for us to follow. He dealt squarely with the devil's shortcuts to fame, power, and riches.

He saw the Faustian "catch" before the Faustian theme had ever been created. The devil said, "All these I will give you, if you will fall down and worship me" (verse 9).

The German poet Johann Wolfgang von Goethe, in his epic literary portrayal of Faust, put Satan's bargain in plain terms. Today we would put it, "Have I got a deal for you!"

Mephistopheles (the devil) promises:

"I'll pledge myself to be thy servant *here,*
  Still at thy beck alert and prompt to be; . . ."

Faust replies: "And how must I thy services repay?"

Mephistopheles wanted more than Faust's word; he wanted it written, sealed in blood:

"In this mood thou mayst venture it. But make
  The compact! I at once will undertake
  To charm thee with mine arts. I'll give thee more
  Than mortal eye hath e'er beheld before. . . ."

And the end of it all, in forecast:

"Vainly he'll seek refreshment, anguish-tost,
  And were he not the devil's by his bond,
  Yet must his soul infallibly be lost!"

(*Harvard Classics*, vol. 19, pp. 64, 65, 71).

The devil's deal is so appealing, so gratifying—the power to have it all, no strings attached, except your soul! The only possible defense is to think like Jesus and Paul: they knew the real purpose and meaning to life.

Jesus put it this way: "Take heed, and beware of all covetousness; for a man's life does not consist in the abundance of his possessions" (Luke 12:15).

Jesus concluded His confrontation with the devil with the immortal answer that works every time: "Away with you, Satan! For it is written, 'You shall worship the Lord your God, and Him only you shall serve'" (Matt. 4:10, NKJV).

To worship God, as we have said in earlier chapters, is to tie our purpose for living with God's purpose for our lives. This knowledge of God's purpose (which is no mystery) defines the Christian's highest purpose for living. It provides the basis for Christian joy!

When any person or group or generation cuts loose from the knowledge of God's purposes for human life, from moral anchors that have been proven wise over the years, we soon have ethical and spiritual uncertainty, then moral bankruptcy. Such is the predicament of the 1990s, the reason for the twilight of joy.

Because of the moral drift, especially of the past 30 years, we should not be surprised that since 1960 violent crime has increased by 560 percent, illegitimate births have climbed by 419 percent, divorce rates have quadrupled, and teenage suicides have jumped by 200 percent.

In reviewing these staggering statistics, former education secretary William Bennett said, "To turn around these numbers, we must engage in the time-honored task of the moral education of our young [and the teaching of] values such as self-restraint, respect for other people, the importance of family, and self-control" (*USA Today*, Mar. 16, 1993).

What has happened is that people, old and young, have not thought first of what God's purposes are for them. They have fallen for the devil's deal: "I will help you 'get it all,' whatever you desire, whatever you feel is right." No wonder the 1990s are cloaked in moral confusion, when dishonesty seems almost right, or at least a way to survive.

Now Paul's word to us. After his experience on the road to

Damascus, he saw ever more clearly what Jesus made forever lucid in His confrontation with the devil: "For me to live is Christ" (Phil. 1:21).

Before Damascus, Paul had it all! Or so he thought. Still a young man, he was highly recognized and respected by the leaders of his church and his nation. He was a member of the Sanhedrin—the Jewish supreme court—no small honor!

He knew how to speak to the Grecian intellectual. Note his remarkable address to the Athenian supreme court, the Areopagus, wherein he converted an Areopagite as well as others to Christianity—in one sermon (Acts 17)! For a wandering Jew to even get a hearing demonstrates some special personal skills and an engaging personality.

He commanded the respect of his former associates, the Jewish leaders, as well as the Roman centurions who tried to keep order while the Jews railed against the early Jewish Christians. His presentations—combining logic, character, and persuasive appeal to the basic human emotions—were worthy of several appearances before magistrates, Roman authorities, and even the rulers of his nation (Acts 22, 23, 24, 25, 28).

In his young manhood, prior to the Damascus Road experience, with the adulation of his countrymen ringing in his ears, Paul was singing: "For me to live is power." He loved the thrill of being on the "inside" where big decisions were made, where power had its luxuries and ego satisfactions. He was given the role as chief persecutor of the hated Christian sect. Later he confessed, "I not only shut up many of the saints in prison, by authority from the chief priests, but when they were put to death I cast my vote against them. And I punished them often in all the synagogues and tried to make them blaspheme; and in raging fury against them, I persecuted them even to foreign cities" (Acts 26:10, 11).

But when he wrote his friendly letter to the Philippians, he was singing a different song. All of his former colleagues (excepting those who had become Christians) had forsaken him. More, they had tried to kill him! Only the fairness of the Roman legal system intervened.

Now after many years of great trial, of awesome achievements in spite of extraordinary physical suffering, of keen disappointments—most everyone thought he was finished. He was old before his time, worn out in service to his Lord. What made it even more difficult for those Romans who respected him was that Paul could leave his miserable cell if only he would renounce his loyalty to that crucified Carpenter and acknowledge Caesar as lord of his life—a very casual commitment, they thought!

But not for Paul. For the past 25 years or more he had lived by a simple motto: "For me to live is Christ." His philosophy of life in one short sentence. His life summarized in a formula!

Remember another famous formula? It appeared first in the mind of Einstein: $E = mc^2$. Later, over Hiroshima and Nagasaki, the truth of that formula exploded and changed the flow of history forever.

Perhaps Paul's formula has changed the world even more than the atomic bomb: I + Christ = life.

What would this world be like if Jesus Christ had lived and died without any disciples to follow and represent Him? No hospitals, no welfare societies, no real dignity of womanhood and children as we know it today in Christian lands—on the list goes.

Think of the awesome exploits of those who have expended themselves for their fellowmen in the name of Jesus: Abram La Rue, Mother Teresa, Tom Dooley, John N. Andrews, Albert Schweitzer, Clarence Emerson, A. T. and D. A. Robinson—the list would fill a book. And it will someday, the book called "the Lamb's book of life"!

Paul's formula really works. Can anyone state his or her philosophy of life in clearer, nobler terms? in fewer words?

If two carbon electrodes are in place and electricity is added, a brilliant light appears. Paul had discovered, long years before writing to the Philippians, that when a Christian and Christ are in the right relationship something wonderful and lasting happens: I + Christ = joy; I + Christ = courage; I + Christ = peace; I + Christ = love.

But he also discovered that most people rewrite their own formula. Some say, I + money = life.

November 21, 1980, was like any other morning in Las

Vegas. In fact, inside the gambling casinos one hardly knows if it is noontime or midnight. The games go on around the clock.

In a way, however, this Friday morning was different. At 7:15 a.m. fire swept through the MGM Grand Hotel. Within minutes, more than 80 people were dead. At the Dunes, a casino directly across the street from the MGM Grand, people occasionally left the gambling tables to watch the fire, only to return shortly to resume their passion. In the Barbary Coast Casino, adjacent to the MGM Grand, women from the MGM, still in their nightgowns, were shooting dice!

A blackjack dealer at the Dunes observed, "There was a flood in Las Vegas a few years ago, and the water swept cars up the street and poured into Caesar's Palace. People just rolled up their pant legs and kept gambling. Men have dropped dead on the floor from heart attacks, and others have been shot. People just look at them and keep playing. When there's construction going on, and all sorts of things are falling, the gamblers just put on hard hats and keep playing.

"There's something about gambling," he said. "People get so wrapped up, they lose sight of everything else" (San Jose *Mercury News*, Nov. 22, 1980).

In chapter 1 we referred to that astonishing book *The Day America Told the Truth.* Chapter 8 is entitled "What Are You Willing to Do for $10 Million? For $2 Million?"

The researchers asked those two questions in every interview. The results, for the $10 million:

25 percent would leave their entire family;

25 percent would leave their church, presumably their faith;

23 percent would become prostitutes for a week or more;

16 percent would leave their spouses;

10 percent would withhold testimony and let a murderer go free;

7 percent would kill a stranger;

4 percent would have a sex-change operation.

All for money! Faust would go for the $10 million and sell his soul! The question for all of us is What is our price?

Of course, there are other formulas that drive people on.

Think of I + pleasure = life. What millions would not do to themselves and others to have one more drink, one more sexual fling, one more cruise, one more chance to really live it up! Family commitments, work responsibilities, health itself—all seem nothing compared to that merry-go-round of pleasure.

But another formula may be more sophisticated: I + status = life. Not necessarily material status this time. But perhaps academic recognition, with its special kind of charm and command. Some achieve their status goals, acing others in finally getting the corner office, or the thicker carpet, or a key to a special washroom! But the end remains the same as the previous mottos: the satisfaction of selfish pursuits, the joy of being number one, if only for their own 15 minutes of fame!

We have not finished Paul's motto. Here is the whole sentence: "For to me to live is Christ, and to die is gain" (Phil. 1:21).

What in the world did Paul mean? Have we been right so far in saying that Paul had found the secret to real joy and peace, that a relationship with Jesus is more rewarding than one with pleasure, status, luxury, or power? If so, why would he prefer death? After all, many thousands commit suicide annually (some say far in excess of 20,000 in the United States) because they too believe that "to die is gain."

Was Paul a weary man who at last had come to the end of his rope? Was he now pessimistic about any chances of coming out of Rome alive? Had he had enough mistreatment by fellow believers and even envious preaching colleagues (see Phil. 1:15-18)? Did he want out—out of this world and into the next? All this and more, of course, has been wrongly read into Paul's dramatic words.

Paul is not simply saying "Life is not worth living." The whole book of Philippians (as we shall see) is a song of joy and peace. He *is* saying that his chief aim in life is to magnify Christ, "whether by life or by death" (verse 20). He was thinking out loud as he wrote: "What would be better, to live or die for Christ?" Paul did not know. But he knew that his friendly Lord knew, and that was enough for Paul.

Paul was not afraid of death. He knew that the next conscious moment after dying, though separated by the sleep of death, would be the face of his Friend, who had never failed him. Either way Paul would win—and that thought undergirded his joy in a miserable Roman prison.

Listen further in verses 23, 24: "I am hard pressed between the two. My desire is to depart and be with Christ, for that is far better. But to remain in the flesh is more necessary on your account."

Tired? Of course he was. Who had given more of himself to others, other than our Lord? But he is not contemplating suicide. His chief concern is the well-being of the young Christian community scattered up and down the Mediterranean basin—and for them he will still bend his energies.

For many years I have been in deepening salute to those five Christian martyrs who were killed by the Auca Indians in Ecuador 40 years ago—the first Caucasians that the scared Aucas had ever seen. We did not know until much after the awful massacre why those five men died.

We had known for years that these brave Christians had guns. They could have used them at last resort. They did not have to die. One of the five made notes inside the plane just before he died: "They came at us with crude spears. We couldn't kill them . . . they would have gone to hell! And so we fired our guns into the air that they might have a chance to hear the gospel."

These five were young, in their 20s. They had wives and children, and they wanted to live as much as anyone reading these lines. But they shot into the air, not into their murderers, for their murderers' sake.

Somehow those Christian martyrs had understood Paul's motto and philosophy of death. For them, beyond any doubt, we + Christ = life. Death was not an awful thought; for them, death with Christ "is gain."

How is it with you? We all face the westering sun, even from the time we are born. Unless Jesus returns within a few years (and He may, you know), all of us will say goodbye to all we cherish. We will leave many unfinished tasks; we won't know how the grandchildren will turn out, or our own children, for that matter.

Will death be "gain" for you? What will be on your mind when you walk into the "shadow of death"?

In his *Legend of the Eagles*, the French writer George d'Esparbes tells of those who made a lasting statement about life and death.

"It was the depth of winter," he writes, "and the French army, pressed on all sides by the Cossacks, had to cross a river. The enemy had destroyed all the bridges, and Napoleon was almost at his wits' end. Suddenly came the order that a bridge of some sort must be thrown across the river, and the men nearest the water, of course, were the first to carry out the almost impossible task. Several were swept away by the furious tide. Others, after a few minutes, sank through cold and exhaustion; but more came, and the work proceeded as fast as possible. At last, the bridge, of sorts, was completed, and the army reached the opposite bank in safety. Then followed a dramatic scene, one of the most horrible recorded in the annals of any nation. When the men who had built the bridge were called out of the water, not one moved. Clinging to pillars, there they stood, silent and motionless— frozen to death. Napoleon, who witnessed the awful scene, could not, in spite of his impassive temperament, restrain his tears" (*The Rotarian,* February 1979, p. 26).

Many go into that rewarding sleep while bearing someone else's burden. Jesus did. Many, following Him, have shared the same fate. Others go cursing Him or their fate.

I think of the Catholic bishop, Romeo Blanchette, of Joliet, Illinois. He was a regular participant on a local call-in talk show, and one day he announced to his radio audience that he had a terminal illness:

"Death [for the faithful] . . . should be a cause for joy. . . . A terminal disease is not something that should bring despair. Rather, it is a reminder to make us reexamine our lives. One day all of us will have to face that moment when we shall have to go from this life into eternity.

"What is terminal?" the bishop asked. "I say everybody is terminal from the day he is born. You start to die when you are born. Some of us are told a little more clearly that it is going to come sooner than others are told. That is a blessing."

As the second hand on the studio clock swept the final minute of the program, the bishop concluded: "The length of time I have left upon the earth depends on the good Lord. I am playing it day by day. . . . I accept it. I hope that we will meet someday in heaven. So goodbye" (Religious News Service, Feb. 28, 1979).

Paul's greatest concern was that we all use every day as a gift and an opportunity: "Only let your manner of life be worthy of the gospel of Christ, so that whether I come and see you or am absent, I may hear of you that you stand firm in one spirit, with one mind striving side by side for the faith of the gospel" (Phil. 1:27).

Such a plea is even more urgent today. As emphasized in the first two chapters, we live in a time of great theological pluralism—which always leads to confusion and emotional disenchantment. The 1990s is not a time of "one spirit, with one mind" that Paul appealed for. All have been exposed to, and some have suffered from, the virus of theological pluralism.

Theological hijacking always creates bewilderment. Topics that should be as clear as the morning sun get clouded over. Even fundamental topics such as When will Jesus return? What kind of people are safe to save? What really happens after death? Does God mean what He says regarding living lives "worthy of the gospel of Christ"? What is Jesus doing now?

When answers to these questions and many others are muddled, when it seems that too many writers and public speakers are speaking a language only recently coined, there is only one result: little or no joy! But when answers to these fundamental questions are resting soundly on time-tested biblical principles, we rediscover Adventist joy.

To make these answers known, to understand unambiguously what God has on His mind for men and women the world over—such today is the specific urgency of Seventh-day Adventists, a special people with a special message for a special time.

They are described in Revelation as those who have learned how to endure amidst life's troubles and distractions; they have learned how to make a life habit of keeping "the commandments of God and the faith of Jesus" (Rev. 4:12).

They have discovered that such life habits do not come forth by merely wishing them so. Neither is such living a matter of seniority, as if we develop lives "worthy of the gospel of Christ" the closer we come to senility!

Such people have learned with Paul: I + Christ = life. They know that life, as we all see it here and now, is a passing shadow. They look at death squarely, realistically. And they stare death down. They do not flinch. Even as their Master from His youth saw life and death in proper perspective—so living that His followers would know how to face their "end of the beginning" both heroically and unselfishly.

In our next chapter we will take a longer look at our friendly Master, our gracious Lord, who became human so that we might better understand both God and ourselves—real reasons for Adventist joy.

Knowing Why Jesus Became Human

5

"In order to fully realize the value of salvation, it is necessary to understand what it cost. In consequence of limited ideas of the sufferings of Christ, many place a low estimate upon the great work of the atonement. . . . Christ consented to die in the sinner's stead, that man, by a life of obedience, might escape the penalty of the law of God. . . . In Christ were united the human and the divine. His mission was to reconcile God and man, to unite the finite with the infinite. This was the only way in which fallen men could be exalted through the merits of the blood of Christ to be partakers of the divine nature. Taking human nature fitted Christ to understand man's trials and sorrows, and all the temptations wherewith he is beset. . . . As the human was upon Him, He felt His need of strength from His Father. He had select places of prayer. . . . In this exercise His holy, human soul was strengthened for the duties and trials of the day. Our Saviour identifies Himself with our needs and weaknesses, in that He became a suppliant, a nightly petitioner, seeking from His Father fresh supplies of strength, to come forth invigorated and refreshed, braced for duty and trial. He is our example in all things" (*Testimonies,* vol. 2, pp. 200-202).

THE first 11 verses of the second chapter of Philippians give us one of the most glorious sweeps of the plan of salvation. Plumbing their depths, along with similar verses elsewhere, brings forth tears of amazement as well as thankfulness. Where in human history has anyone ever given up so much for so many ungrateful people—all the while, knowing in advance that billions of people would reject Him!

Look at Jesus, equal with God—His divinity (verse 6). Observe Him as He "emptied himself, taking the form of a servant, being born in the likeness of men" (verse 7)—His humanity.

Watch Him grow up as any baby boy must—His mysterious incarnation. Behold Him as a servant-leader—humanity's Example. Contemplate Him on the cross—His sacrificial atonement and humanity's Saviour. Turn your eyes to the soon-to-be future, to His glorious exaltation when "every knee" shall bow (verse 10)—still in His humanity, but forever the answer to all misapprehensions, false charges, and lies about the character of God. The big picture—it's all here in Paul's second chapter.

The questions pour forth: Why would God want to do this? Why did He have to? What was He trying to prove? What did He gain? The answers are found, of course, in the unfolding of the great controversy between Christ and Satan.

Before we look in on this cosmic conflict that affects everyone today, we should note why Paul brought this deep and crucial subject into his pastoral letter to the Philippians. After all, Paul was not developing a Bible doctrine course on the nature and work of Christ, nor was he countering some great heresy.

In the first chapter to the Philippians, Paul shared with the local church his concern regarding spiritual rivalries and doctrinal divisions caused by preachers on ego trips (see verses 15, 16). In chapter 2 he continues his concern with this appeal: "Do nothing from selfishness or conceit, but in humility count others better than yourselves" (verse 3). Apparently, some Philippians thought they could be Christians while still proud, competitive, and contentious.

So Paul, knowing that such strife could destroy the credibility of Christianity, lifted his readers in a soaring, fourfold appeal to unity, humbleness, helpfulness, and unselfishness (see verses 1, 2).

But Paul knew better than to exhort only. He gave his readers an illustration. He turned their eyes toward Jesus as the example and goal of how the Philippians should behave, among themselves and to persons outside the church. The intensity of Philippians 2, its mind-stretching, heart-tugging focus on the incredible cascade of eternal love poured out in Jesus' becoming man, compares with the Matterhorn among mountains or Chartres among cathedrals.

Paul is simply saying, as he had on numerous other occasions, that to be one of His, to participate in the fellowship of the Holy Spirit, the Christian must have the mind of Jesus—that is, His disposition, attitudes, and distinctive qualities of temperament. The Christian's high privilege, Paul says, is to reflect the mind of Jesus—the same self-emptying humility, the same commitment, serving others regardless of personal loss.

Andrew Murray, a much-sought speaker and writer almost a century ago, was awed by this chapter and asked: "And does Paul, and do the Scriptures, and does God really expect this of us? Why not? Or rather, how can they expect anything else? They know indeed the fearful power of pride and the old Adam in our nature. But they know also that Christ has redeemed us not only from the curse but from the power of sin, and that He gives us His resurrection life and power to enable us to live as He did on earth. They say that He is not only our Surety, but our Example also; so that we not only live through Him, but like Him. And further, not only Example but also our Head, who lives in us, and continues in us the life He once led on earth. With such a Christ, and such a plan of redemption, can it be otherwise? The follower of Christ must have the same mind as was in Christ; he must especially be like Him in His humility" (*Like Christ* [Minneapolis: Bethany Fellowship, Inc., 1974], p. 139).

Let us do what Paul did. Instead of focusing on problems within Philippi (or people problems within our own local church), let us fasten our gaze on Jesus. Paul had discovered that the story of Jesus, rightly told, becomes the most compelling incentive, the strongest motivation, to change self-oriented, independent, and competitive church members into genuine sons and daughters of God.

So we ask, Why did Jesus "empty" Himself and come to earth? Was it worth it? How will we know if He succeeded?

The answers take us back, before the creation of this world. Back to that time when "there was war in heaven" (Rev. 12:7). Right, war in heaven! "A third of the stars [angels]" (Rev. 12:4) rebelled, led by the chief rebel, "the Devil and Satan, the deceiver of the whole world" (verse 9).

And so the great controversy between God and Satan developed. Happily, we are not left in darkness regarding how the conflict ends. John the revelator tells us that after millennia of struggles to the death, after Satan has done all he can to deceive the universe regarding the wisdom and judgment of God, "the loud voice of a great multitude in heaven [is heard] crying, 'Hallelujah! Salvation and glory and power belong to our God, for his judgments are true and just'" (Rev. 19:1, 2).

In this ringing reaffirmation that concludes the controversy there lies a clue as to what the conflict was all about. We hear the echoes of Satan's charges: "God has been unfair! He is severe and arbitrary!" Hence, the great controversy over who has been right, our friendly God or the great deceiver, ends only when God's onlooking universe is convinced that He is worth our admiration, our trust, our love!

Who is Satan? How could anyone dare challenge God and be believable? What has been his "line" ever since he founded his beachhead on Planet Earth and tried to wrest this world from God forever?

Questions about God are also raised: What kind of God runs this universe? Is He worth trusting? Why didn't He obliterate Satan in the beginning and thus head off the unspeakable anguish that followed? What is God's convincing and final answer to Satan's charges?

First, Satan. The revelator described him as "the Devil [literally, "the one who thrusts through"] and Satan [literally, "the adversary"] the deceiver of the whole world" (Rev. 12:9), "that ancient serpent" (Rev. 20:2). Jesus called him "a murderer from the beginning. . . . He is a liar and the father of lies" (John 8:44).

Originally, Satan was Lucifer, or "Day Star, son of Dawn" (Isa. 14:12)—the first of all created beings. He was created in "perfection, full of wisdom and perfect in beauty" (Eze. 28:12); "You were blameless in your ways from the day you were created, till iniquity was found in you" (verse 15).

The nature of this "iniquity" is depicted as a "proud" heart. The desire to be number one "corrupted your wisdom for the sake of your splendor" (verse 17).

Insane as the idea is, Lucifer (Satan) "said in [his] heart, 'I will ascend to heaven; above the stars of God I will set my throne on high; . . . I will ascend above the heights of the clouds, I will make myself like the Most High'" (Isa. 14:13, 14).

Satan coveted God's glory and authority. He began the process of turning the allegiance of the angels from God toward himself. He especially coveted, and later hated, the place and person of that Member of the Godhead later to be known as Jesus, the Christ, who perhaps had already begun His long descent as Creation's Mediator in the form of the archangel Michael (see Dan. 10:12, 13; 12:1; 1 Thess. 4:16; Jude 9).

Covetousness, jealousy, cunning deception, and open rebellion—it was all there, even in heaven. (And that sad decline has been repeated millions of times since.) Satan's sinister charges, the subtle lies ("liar from the beginning"), were not easily met, as all deception and falsehood ever since have been difficult to meet because of their very nature.

What has Satan lied about? What have been his deceptions? He lied about the character of God, about the nature of sin, and the supposed independent potential of created beings. He charged that God's law of love was, in fact, an inverted law of subtle selfishness—that God asked for loyalty and obedience, but for Himself He does not and would not exercise self-denial and a spirit of sacrifice. Further, Satan has charged, with beguiling logic, that God is the author of sin, suffering, and death. On top of everything else, he has sold the lie that God has made laws that cannot be obeyed by created beings, even if they tried. And if they tried, they would forever limit their full potential!

Now we begin to see how the story of Jesus as set forth in the second chapter of Philippians is so important in getting an understanding of how God has countered Satan's lies and charges.

The unfolding of Satan's lies and their bitter consequences presented God with a colossal challenge: How could He get a favorable hearing? How could He present the "whole truth" about who He really was? How could He restore human rebels who had been infected morally and depraved physically by their rebellion?

The answers to these questions appear in passages throughout the Bible, as well as in the second chapter of Philippians. Jesus revealed (1) what God is truly like (John 14:9), (2) what humanity originally was created to be like (Gen. 1:26), and (3) what humanity could expect to be like when submitted to Him as their friendly Redeemer (Rom. 8:29). Theologians have described this work in terms such as Sacrifice, Teacher, and Example, as well as Saviour, Redeemer, and Lord.

As we learned in the first chapter of Philippians and in each succeeding chapter, Paul sets before his readers their high destiny. Christians have the towering honor of being known, by the power of their enabling Lord, as people "who approve what is excellent," people who are "pure and blameless for the day of Christ" (Phil. 1:10); people whose "manner of life [is] worthy of the gospel of Christ" (verse 27).

Thus, Christ's followers demonstrate to this world and to the onlooking universe two undeniable facts: (1) through His enabling grace obedience is possible, and (2) such loyalty produces gracious, trustworthy, humble, loving men and women who glorify and vindicate God's wisdom and government. (See Eze. 36:21-27; 2 Cor. 4:5-7, 10, 11; Eph. 1:4, 6, 12; 3:8-21; Titus 2:11-13; 3:5-7; 2 Peter 3:11-14.)

In the process His followers on earth will have discovered that what the universe thinks about God is even more important than their own personal salvation. Their primary motivation for Christian discipleship is a desire to help God clarify the issues in the great controversy rather than a focus on "getting themselves saved." In brief, what happens to God becomes more important than what happens to them! That's how friends really think!

What we are discussing is not merely a theological exercise. Hardly! Paul's point in Philippians is that church members must clearly understand why Jesus came to earth—participating in the human genetic stream as all babies do—and why He lived the way He did.

Perhaps this is why my favorite author wrote: "In order to grow in grace and in the knowledge of Christ, it is essential that you meditate much upon the great themes of redemption. You should ask yourself why Christ has taken humanity upon Himself, why He suffered upon the cross, why He bore the sins of men, why He was made sin and righteousness for us. You should study to know why He ascended to heaven in the nature of man, and what is His work for us today. . . . We think that we are familiar with the character of Christ, and we do not realize how much is to be gained by the study of our glorious Pattern. We take it for granted that we know all about Him, and yet we do not comprehend His character or mission" (*Signs of the Times*, Dec. 1, 1890).

In the context of Philippians 2 and with the last exhortation in mind, let's ever so briefly survey the reasons, in view of the great controversy, why Jesus came to this earth.

1. **He came to reveal the Father.** "He reflects the glory of God [His character] and bears the very stamp of his nature" (Heb. 1:3). "The Word became flesh and dwelt among us, full of grace and truth; we have beheld his glory, glory as of the only Son from the Father" (John 1:14).

"Christ exalted the character of God, attributing to Him the praise and giving to Him the credit, of the whole purpose of His own mission on earth—to set men right through the revelation of God. . . . When the object of His mission was attained—the revelation of God to the world—the Son of God announced that His work was accomplished, and that the character of the Father was made manifest to men" (*Signs of the Times*, Jan. 20, 1890; see also *The Desire of Ages*, p. 19).

2. **Jesus came to silence the accusations of Satan.** These include:

   a. God had made a law that nobody could keep after the disobedience of Adam (see Manuscript 1, 1892, in *Review and Herald*, June 17, 1976; *The Faith I Live By*, p. 114).

   b. God's law is really a law of selfishness (see *The Desire of Ages*, p. 24).

   c. God Himself is the author of sin, suffering, and death (see *The Desire of Ages*, p. 24).

   d. God's justice destroys His mercy; sin (rebellion) cannot be forgiven (see *The Desire of Ages*, p. 762).

   e. God was so lofty and imperial that He would do nothing for so insignificant a creature as man (see *Signs of the*

Times, Jan. 20, 1890).

    f. God did not have sufficient love for His creatures to exercise the same self-denial and sacrifice He required from them (see *Patriarchs and Prophets*, p. 70).

    3. **Jesus came to give fallen men and women an example of obedience.** "Christ also suffered for us, leaving us an example, that ye should follow his steps" (1 Peter 2:21, KJV; see also John 13:15; 2 Cor. 4:10). "And every man that hath this hope in him purifieth himself, even as he is pure" (1 John 3:3, KJV). "He that doeth righteousness is righteous, even as he is righteous" (verse 7, KJV). "He that saith he abideth in him ought himself also so to walk, even as he walked" (1 John 2:6, KJV).

    "In Him was found the perfect ideal. To reveal this ideal as the only true standard for attainment; to show what every human being might become; what, through the indwelling of humanity by divinity, all who received Him would become—for this, Christ came to the world. He came to show how men are to be trained as befits the sons of God; how on earth they are to practice the principles and to live the life of heaven" (*Education*, pp. 73, 74; see also *The Desire of Ages*, pp. 49, 671, 762).

    4. **Jesus came to be humanity's righteousness.** "Through Jesus, God's mercy was manifested to men; but mercy does not set aside justice. . . . The law requires righteousness—a righteous life, a perfect character; and this man has not to give. He cannot meet the claims of God's holy law. But Christ, coming to the earth as man, lived a holy life, and developed a perfect character. These He offers as a free gift to all who will receive them. His life stands for the life of men. Thus they have remission of sins that are past, through the forbearance of God. More than this, Christ imbues men with the attributes of God. He builds up the human character after the similitude of the divine character, a goodly fabric of spiritual strength and beauty. Thus the very righteousness of the law is fulfilled in the believer in Christ. God can 'be just and the justifier of him which believeth in Jesus' (Rom. 3:26). . . .

    "By His life and His death, Christ proved that God's justice did not destroy His mercy, but that sin could be forgiven, and that the law is righteous, and can be perfectly obeyed. Satan's charges were refuted. God had given men unmistakable evidence of His love" (*The Desire of Ages*, p. 762).

If space would allow, we would study additional reasons Jesus came to earth as He did, as any baby would be born, partaking of the genetic bloodstream as other babies do, partaking of "the same nature. . . . Therefore he had to be made like his brethren in every respect" (Heb. 2:14, 17; see also *The Desire of Ages*, p. 49).

Each one of the many reasons begs for pause and reflection! Each one deserves a chapter of its own, showing how it fills in more detail in the great controversy theme.

Understanding why Jesus came to earth overwhelmed Paul as it does anyone who grasps even glimpses of what His coming to earth as a human being means.

And then to think what it meant to Jesus, to the Father, and to the Holy Spirit. They were giving up a relationship that never again would be exactly the same—even after Jesus returned to heaven (see 1 Cor. 15:28; *The Desire of Ages*, p. 832). Evermore Jesus is confined within time and space, carrying the limitations of human nature. Can anyone calculate the cost? And the inherent risk? (See *The Desire of Ages*, p. 49.) Yet God thought you and I were worth it. Cause for joy, isn't it?

Now we can better understand why Paul says to us today, Let that mind of Jesus—that mind that thought and felt and acted as our friendly Lord, the humble Servant, the great Forgiver, the disciplined Surety, the patient Teacher, the faithful Son, the trusted Companion—let that mind, His mind, be in us also. Paul is projecting more than an ideal; his words reflect His promise—for that was one of our Lord's reasons for coming to Planet Earth.

The well-being of the universe has been wrenched and severely jeopardized from the beginning by those who thought that autonomous, independent judgment and ambitious self-glory were more rewarding than self-denial, unity of spirit, and deferment to others. Jesus has shown us that God withholds no good thing from His creation—that love, peace, and joy spring from God's own self-sacrifice and humility. Should His creation, especially those who call Him Lord, give back less?

As we noted in chapter 3, He now waits for people who grasp

the issues in the great controversy. Again, my favorite author: "When Christ shall come, our vile bodies are to be changed, made like His glorious body; but the vile character will not be made holy then. The transformation of character must take place before His coming, our natures must be pure and holy; we must have the mind of Christ, that He may behold with pleasure His image reflected upon our souls" (*Our High Calling*, p. 278).

For those who let that seed grow so that the mind of Jesus is reflected in their thoughts and acts—for those men and women, life will be aglow with joy. This will become even clearer as we study our way through Philippians and Colossians.

Experiencing God's Power

6

"Therefore [in view of Christ's example and ministry] . . . work out your own salvation with fear and trembling; for God is at work in you, both to will and to work for his good pleasure. Do all things without grumbling or questioning, that you may be blameless and innocent, children of God without blemish in the midst of a crooked and perverse generation, among whom you shine as lights in the world" (Phil. 2:12-15). "Be found in him, not having a righteousness of [your] own, based on law, but that which is through faith in Christ, the righteousness from God that depends on faith" (Phil. 3:9).

IF A Christian should want to know anything above all else, surely it would be what Paul refers to in these verses as God's "good pleasure." God's "good pleasure" is our salvation! Restoring His universe in such a way that no angel or human being would ever again want to think a rebellious thought—that would be God's good pleasure! Enjoying the eternal security of all His creation—that would be God's good pleasure!

In his first letter to the Thessalonians, Paul spelled out again what God's good pleasure is: "You learned from us how you ought to live and to please God, just as you are doing, you do so more and more. . . . This is the will of God, your sanctification. . . . For God has not called us for uncleanness, but in holiness. Therefore whoever disregards this, disregards not man but God, who gives his Holy Spirit to you" (1 Thess. 4:1-8).

Peter caught the same vision of God's good pleasure: "As obedient children, do not be conformed to the passions of your former ignorance, but as he who called you is holy, be holy yourselves in all your conduct; since it is written, 'You shall be holy, for I am holy.' And if you invoke as Father him who judges each one impartially according to his deeds, conduct yourselves with fear throughout the time of your exile" (1 Peter 1:14-17).

Is this language being made clear these days? Many voices surrounding us in the past 30 years, both in the Adventist Church and elsewhere, insist that to focus on sanctification as a significant part of the salvation process is to retreat to Rome and to works salvation. For them, to ask for holy lives as part of the gospel message is to lay a crushing burden on "saved" Christians. This burden, they say, leads to frustration, perhaps even despair. After all, who is holy? Or perfect?

Is God asking the impossible when He calls us to "work out" our salvation—to "be holy"—as His will for us?

Interestingly, to suggest that God is asking the impossible is to repeat exactly what Satan has been saying from the beginning—and what he has artfully confused the minds of many professed Christians to believe! Observe: "Through defects in the character, Satan works to gain control of the whole mind, and he knows that if these defects are cherished, he will succeed. Therefore he is constantly seeking to deceive the followers of Christ with his fatal sophistry that it is impossible for them to overcome" (*The Great Controversy*, p. 489).

"Satan has asserted that men could not keep the commandments of God. To prove that they could, Christ became a man, and lived a life of perfect obedience, an evidence to sinful human beings, to the worlds unfallen, and to the heavenly angels, that man could keep God's law through the divine power that is abundantly provided for all that believe. In order to reveal God to the world, to demonstrate as true that which Satan has denied, Christ volunteered to take humanity, and in His power, humanity can obey God" (*Signs of the Times*, May 10, 1899).

Many Christians have found psychological relief in Satan's lies; too often we believe in our heads what our hearts want to believe. The theological arguments of these Christians go in several directions: 1. The cross of Christ canceled the demands of the law, placing all believers under grace. 2. Trying to keep the law is unnecessary because Jesus kept the law for us. 3. Trying to keep the law is a foolish attempt because overcoming sin is impossible while we still live in sinful flesh. 4. Trying to keep the law leads either to frustration or legalism.

However, these theological excuses are attempts to evade the clear call of Jesus: "Every one then who hears these words of mine and does them will be like a wise man who built his house upon the rock" (Matt. 7:24).

Satan has done his work well—but God has had His people through the years who have proven Satan wrong. Such people listen to biblical writers rather than to preachers and theologians who build their arguments on faulty philosophical and theological presuppositions.

In later chapters we will discuss why even Christians buy Satan's lies that obedience and overcoming sin are impossible. For now, let us find peace in listening to Paul and other Bible writers who give a clear alternative to Satan's charges and insinuations. Only by listening to Paul chapter by chapter (not a verse here out of context and then another from another context) will we know the truth about God's good pleasure.

Let the Bible speak to you. Hear what Paul heard. Remove the filters of theological debate and commentaries. Let the simple words speak directly, personally, quietly, to your soul. Read the verses again that begin this chapter.

Ponder what Jesus meant when He said, "Strive to enter by the narrow door" (Luke 13:24). Selfish, rebellious people cannot inherit the kingdom of God because they strive for what they consider to be more important than "the narrow door." That is the clearest, most consistent bottom line of Scripture, hammered home from Genesis to Revelation. Jesus came to help us through that "narrow door." That is why His name is Jesus, "for he will save his people *from* their sins" (Matt. 1:21)—not in them.

But just saying this indeed raises the question How? We all know how persistently weak we all are, how far short we are from even our own highest standards, never mind our Lord's. Is it a matter of developing our willpower—of simply striving harder? No! Never! God has given us a better plan—a plan that works whenever we buy into it!

That is why the Holy Spirit led Peter to write: "His divine power has granted to us all things that pertain to life and godliness, through the knowledge of him who called us to his own glory and excellence, by which he has granted to us his precious and very great promises, that through these you may escape from the corruption that is in the world because of passion, and become partakers of the divine nature" (2 Peter 1:3, 4).

Note that God does not push you out of the driver's seat. He does not do the driving for you, as the Greyhound bus ad reads! His terrific goal for you is to make you into a responsible, predictable, trustworthy driver of your life—a person safe to save, made safe by His continuing grace.

This theme is throughout the Bible. Listen to Paul challenge the Ephesians: "That according to the riches of his glory he may grant you to be strengthened with might through his Spirit in the inner man" (Eph. 3:16).

Here in the second chapter of Philippians we are given the formula of how we are "strengthened with might"—how we become overcomers: *Our will + God's grace = overcomers.* In this life? Absolutely! There is no second chance after death—we are having our renewed chances every day we wake up. In this life we seal our destiny. It's written throughout Scripture: "He who conquers shall be clad thus in white garments, and I will not blot his name out of the book of life" (Rev. 3:5). "He who conquers, I will grant him to sit with me on my throne, as I myself conquered" (verse 21).

Here is a sampling of scores of confirming declarations: "When he comes, he is not to cleanse us of our sins, to remove from us the defects in our characters, or to cure us of the infirmities of our tempers and dispositions. If wrought for us at all, this work will all be accomplished before that time. When the Lord comes, those who are holy will be holy still. Those who have preserved their bodies and spirits in holiness, in sanctification and honor, will then receive the finishing touch of immortality. But those who are unjust, unsanctified, and filthy will remain so forever. No work will then be done for them to remove their defects and give them holy characters. . . . This is all to be done in these hours of probation. It is *now* that this work is to be accomplished for us. . . .

"As we lay hold upon the truth of God, its influence affects us. It elevates us and removes from us every imperfection and sin, of whatever nature. . . . The Spirit of God should have perfect control of us, influencing us in all our actions. If we have a right hold on Heaven, a right hold of the power that is from above, we shall feel the sanctifying influence of the Spirit of God upon our hearts" (*Testimonies*, vol. 2, pp. 355, 356).

Paul's formula is a fundamental biblical principle: *Our will + God's grace = overcomers.*

Look at it again in Philippians 2:12, 13: "Work out your own salvation" + God is at work in you = "His good pleasure" (our salvation).

Our part is spelled out in such texts as: "strive" (Luke 13:24; Heb. 4:11); "Put off the old man" (Col. 3:9, KJV); "Lay aside every weight . . . run with patience" (Heb. 12:1, KJV); "Resist the devil" (James 4:7, KJV); "Abide in me." "Keep my commandments" (John 15:4, 10, KJV). The list of such texts is very long.

God's part is to provide "grace to help in time of need" (Heb. 4:16, KJV). This grace is provided "through his Spirit" (Eph. 3:16), "by the power at work within us" (verse 20). Many texts remind us that God "is able to strengthen you" (Rom. 16:25); He "is able to keep you from falling" (Jude 24).

A clear description of how Paul's formula works in our lives is found in that delightful book *Messages to Young People:* "While these youth were working out their own salvation, God was working in them to will and to do of His good pleasure. Here are revealed the conditions of success. To make God's grace our own, we must act our part. The Lord does not propose to perform for us either the willing or the doing. His grace is given to work in us to will and to do, but never as a substitute for our effort. Our souls are to be aroused to cooperate. The Holy Spirit works in us, that we may work out our own salvation. This is the practical lesson the Holy Spirit is striving to teach us" (p. 147).

To highlight the divine-human co-op plan, again my favorite author could not be clearer: "The work of gaining salvation is one of copartnership, a joint operation. There is to be cooperation between God and the repentant sinner. This is necessary for the formation of right principles in the character. Man is to make earnest efforts to overcome that which hinders him from attaining to perfection. But he is wholly dependent upon God for success. Human effort of itself is not sufficient. Without the aid of divine power it avails nothing. God works and man works. Resistance of temptation must come from man, who must draw his power from God. . . . He must study the Word of God, learning its meaning and obeying its precepts. Thus he may reach the standard of Christian excellence. Day by day God works with him, perfecting the character that is to stand in the day of final test. And day by day the believer is working out before men and angels a sublime experiment, showing what the gospel can do for fallen human beings" (*The Acts of the Apostles*, pp. 482, 483).

Paul uses an interesting phrase, "work . . . with fear and trembling." What could he mean—"with fear and trembling"? For one thing, Paul is not throwing a gray cloud over the working, striving Christian. Nor is he placing the Christian in the impossible position of Sisyphus—always rolling the rock that almost makes the top of the hill but always rolls back again.

When God cooperates with our best efforts, no one needs to fear failure. God always lives up to His promises. He will never grow weary of picking us up, any more than a parent grows impatient with his child learning to walk.

However, in a special sense, fear has its place in working out our salvation. "God does not bid you fear that He will fail to fulfill His promises, that His patience will weary, or His compassion be found wanting. Fear lest your will shall not be held in subjection to Christ's will, lest your hereditary and cultivated traits of character shall control your life. . . . Fear lest self shall interpose between your soul and the great Master Worker. Fear lest self-will shall mar the high purpose that through you God desires to accomplish. Fear to trust to your own strength, fear to withdraw your hand from the hand of Christ and attempt to walk life's pathway without His abiding presence" (*Christ's Object Lessons*, p. 161).

This life of cooperation with the mind and power of God, this working out of God's "good pleasure," this life of abiding in Christ, is what Paul calls "the righteousness from God that depends on faith" (Phil. 3:9).

Paul had seen the futility of working out a form of "righteousness" that depended on ritual performance and human effort alone. Before his conversion he had misunderstood what the plan of redemption was aiming at. After Damascus he saw that God did not desire external performance as evidence that His people were loyal: "For I desire steadfast love and not sacrifice, the knowledge of God, rather than burnt offerings" (Hosea 6:6).

Probably no one ever wanted righteousness more than Paul, even before he met Jesus on the Damascus road. But he came to reject any so-called righteousness "of my own" (Phil. 3:9) because he saw that it led only to pride, self-sufficiency, and the eclipse of love. What Paul saw in the gospel, as well as all young Christians such as Stephen, was a totally different approach to righteousness that resonated the deepest messages of the Old Testament. He finally understood faith and how it relates to the "righteousness from God." (There will be more about New Testament faith in chapter 11.)

Like a flash of lightning, Paul saw that "the righteousness which Christ taught is conformity of heart and life to the revealed will of God. Sinful men can become righteous only as they have faith in God and maintain a vital connection with Him. Then true godliness will elevate the thoughts and ennoble the life. Then the external forms of religion accord with the Christian's inward purity" (*The Desire of Ages*, p. 310).

The key thought, the open secret, to Paul's salvation formula regarding our part and God's part in working out our salvation is the work of the Holy Spirit, the indwelling energizer. Strange to say, the primary function of the Holy Spirit has been rarely described throughout the Christian era! Along with His work as the convincer of sin, as the helpful tutor as we read the Bible, His highest purpose, toward which all other functions focus, is to reproduce in us the character of Jesus. This is the only way the

Holy Spirit (or anyone else) can truly witness to Jesus: "The Spirit of truth, who proceeds from the Father, he will bear witness to me" (John 15:26).

Perhaps it has never been stated more clearly than in the following quotation: "The Holy Spirit is the breath of spiritual life in the soul. The impartation of the Spirit is the impartation of the life of Christ. It imbues the receiver with the attributes of Christ. Only those who are thus taught of God, those who possess the inward working of the Spirit, and in whose life the Christ-life is manifested, are we to stand as representative men" (*The Desire of Ages*, p. 805).

Never will the time come when we will no longer need the grace of God, as manifested in the friendly energy of the Holy Spirit. Until the Christian dies, or until Jesus returns, every genuine, faithful Christian will feel the appeal of sin, the tug of Satan, even as Jesus did—even to the end of His earthly life.

Our daily challenge will be to subdue every prompting to serve selfish interests, to leave them conquered on the battlefield—even as Jesus did, even as many God-loving people have done in every generation since Creation. This quotation may give us added courage: "Some few in every generation from Adam resisted his every artifice and stood forth as noble representatives of what it was in the power of man to do and to be—Christ working with human efforts, helping man in overcoming the power of Satan. Enoch and Elijah are the correct representatives of what the race might be through faith in Jesus Christ if they chose to be. Satan was greatly disturbed because these noble, holy men stood untainted amid the moral pollution surrounding them, perfected righteous characters, and were accounted worthy for translation to heaven" (*Review and Herald*, Mar. 3, 1874).

In later chapters we will study in more depth Paul's counsel regarding the salvation formula that describes the divine-human co-op plan. Human weakness unites resolutely with divine strength—and faith sings, "Thank God for the victory!" Such will be the growing experience of the Christian who lets God work out "the righteousness from God that depends on faith." I can't think of any better cause for joy—He's got it all figured out. His formula is more powerful than $E = mc^2$!

Philippians 3:12-21

Keeping the Main Thing the Main Thing

7

"Higher than the highest human thought can reach is God's ideal for His children. Godliness—godlikeness—is the goal to be reached. Before the student there is opened a path of continual progress. He has an object to achieve, a standard to attain, that includes everything good, and pure, and noble. He will advance as fast and as far as possible in every branch of true knowledge. But his efforts will be directed to objects as much higher than mere selfish and temporal interests as the heavens are higher than the earth" *(Education,* pp. 18, 19).

FOR the past five months I have been recovering from two herniated discs. For weeks I have been flat on my back; lately I have had my right foot higher than my keyboard, trying to write this book. At other times I am with my kind and careful physical therapist, inching along together, reducing pain and stretching for lost strength in my strangely numb but painful right leg. Before meeting Phil, I wondered at times if the pain would ever go away or if I would ever return to anything that approached normal living.

On Phil's wall is a poster, a Nike ad: "There is no finish line." Three times a week, for months, I contemplated that message—then it hit me: I knew I had my lead into this seventh chapter! That poster kept me on target, even when wondering whether I would ever walk again without a cane!

"No finish line." Paul came to know this remarkable concept after he met his Friend along the Damascus road. Before Damascus he thought he had it all—wrapped up in prestige and power. In a way, he did have the future wrapped up—totally secure in his "homemade righteousness."

In fact, "as to righteousness under the law," he and his friends considered him "blameless" (Phil. 3:6). But after the meeting with his Friend, his world turned upside down. He shifted from the security of righteousness gained by conforming to legal requirements to "the surpassing worth of knowing Christ Jesus my Lord" (verse 8).

The present became a joy; the future, a magnificent magnet of compelling hope. Listen to his future: "That I may know him and the power of his resurrection, and may share his sufferings, becoming like him in his death, that if possible I may attain the resurrection from the dead" (verses 10, 11). Is such a future the main thing in your life?

I have read somewhere that driving at a speed of 30 miles an hour one can absorb only seven words from a billboard. People pay big money to catch your attention—with only a few words!

How about a bumper sticker? They seem countless. Some make sense; some you wish you had not read! Sometimes we have to get very close to get the point, such as the one that read: "The main thing is to keep the main thing the main thing."

What is the main thing in life for you? What is the main thing you do when you have some time for yourself? In your education? In your marriage? With your children? With your money?

Paul's "main thing" after Damascus: to do "one thing . . . forgetting what lies behind and straining forward to what lies ahead, I press on toward the goal for the prize of the upward call of God in Christ Jesus" (verses 13, 14). What does Paul mean? So much misunderstanding has occurred through the centuries as to what Paul meant!

First of all, Paul is reemphasizing the harvest principle, which interlaces his many letters. We plant hard, dry corn seeds and then we nurture them to "press on" toward the goal for which they were planted. Perfect corn seeds are expected to mature, to produce a harvest—if they do not keep growing, they cease to be "perfect." They do not reach "the goal, the prize." They may have started well, but they missed the point of how to remain perfect in the eyes of their planters.

Second, Paul is passing on an open secret of successful people, certainly the principle undergirding joyful Christians: forget the past! Easier said than done, right?

The Greek word we translate "forgetting" is an ancient athletic term that describes a runner who surpasses another. The athlete knows that he must not be distracted by looking over his shoulders—he must keep his eyes on the prize ahead. The Greek term is intensive—*completely* forgetting!

Nothing seems to steal joy quicker than to rehearse the past! Wasted moments, remorse for unkindness, lies (known or unknown by others), shame brought to your loved ones—on the list goes. The load can get heavy. But the Christian believes his Friend—all these things are forgiven! Especially as He helps us to make right the wrongs we have done. In addition, those neural paths that led us into those moral quagmires are being redirected by the Holy Spirit. The past can teach us all something—but it is not to be "called up" as one would a computer file.

Paul is also saying to forget all those spiritual crutches that we once used to curry God's favor. Forget the idea that we are good because we are not really bad! Forget the idea that we can be Christians without knowing, in a trusting, experiential way, Jesus as our personal Saviour from sin!

Paul strongly urges us to completely forget those depressing, energy-sapping memories—one does that by keeping the eyes focused on the "upward call of God in Christ Jesus" (verse 14).

Third, Paul reminds us that this focus on the "goal for the prize of the upward call" is not a once-a-week affair—say, when in church. The Greek word translated "press" depicts a runner or a chariot racer who leans into the race, stretching every muscle, never giving up, but keeping his eye on his prize. The word is similar in meaning to other words we have used in previous chapters, such as "strive," "work out," and "abide." Paul made a life habit of leaning into the future, with his eyes zoomed in on his goal—honoring God, doing His service.

Jesus was like that—He had a goal and a plan for each day. He showed us that the Christian life cannot be lived in neutral. Walking as Jesus walked requires decision-making daily. The same eagerness, the same anticipation, that kept Jesus and Paul and a host of saints facing the future with enthusiasm is ours to possess. Too many Christians look back, even to the moment when they were "saved." That seems to be their security! They don't understand the joy of growing up, the excitement of letting God finish what He started (Phil. 1:6). They don't "keep pressing on."

The fourth point Paul makes in these verses is that the emphasis is on direction, not perfection, Perfection is a word that must be used carefully because of its rampant abuse. We could very well present the gospel and the whole intent of the Bible without using this word.

Biblical perfection does not refer to a state in which a person is beyond temptation or the possibility of sin, any more than Jesus was immune to temptation and self-indulgence. Neither does the Bible mean that the perfection set before Christians suggests a state of physical and mental accomplishment in which no illnesses arise or no mental mistakes (such as in mathematics) are made.

For the Greek word often translated "perfection," many English translations interchange such terms as "maturity" or "completeness." But what does biblical perfection or maturity or completeness mean? Those words sound ominous, even scary.

Perhaps a helpful understanding of the biblical concept of perfection may be obtained from the following quotation: "Moral perfection is required of all. Never should we lower the standard of righteousness in order to accommodate inherited or cultivated tendencies to wrongdoing. We need to understand that imperfection of character is sin. . . . The heavenly intelligences will work with the human agent who seeks with determined faith that perfection of character which will reach out to perfection in action" (*Christ's Object Lessons*, pp. 330-332).

Perfection, as understood in the above quotation, is in contrast to the concept of perfectionism. The latter term, emphasizing an absolute point beyond which there is no need for further development, grows out of Grecian philosophy, not the Bible. Perfection in the biblical sense is simply Christlikeness.

In the third chapter of his Philippian letter, Paul is amplifying the biblical description of what "perfect" people are like: they keep facing the future with hope, they keep growing, they keep letting God work out His good pleasure in their lives. They never give up! They hang tough, regardless of earthly circumstances!

Then Paul says something very wistful, perhaps springing from what he had noticed in the early Christian church: some did not keep pressing on, some felt that they had already attained, some put their religious experience into neutral. And they all began to lose what they had.

Perhaps we all have experienced "losing what we had." It seems that we can lose in an hour what had taken months, perhaps years, to gain. Not a fair trade—but such is the nature of growth. Some plants are that way—they receive months of careful attention, but after careless neglect for a few days they are barely retrievable. However, the good news is that, no matter how much neglect we allow to settle in, God has marvelous ways to "restore to you the years that the locust hath eaten" (Joel 2:25, KJV). Our friendly Lord has not turned one request down—and won't!

I remember the day when I took my children to the battlefield at Saratoga, New York. We had a special reason to see this battlefield and its special, large obelisk with four niches in its corners. This monument is dedicated to four generals of the American Continental Army who were in command of that decisive Colonial victory—the turning point of the American Revolution.

The four men were Gates, Schuyler, Morgan, and Arnold. General Gates was supreme commander during the battle for Saratoga, but the battle would have been lost if he had not been aided late in the day by the dashing leadership of Benedict Arnold. Arnold did more with his 3,000 men than Gates did with his 11,000. General Arnold was second only to George Washington in the eyes of the Continental soldier.

But on that monument today you will find the names and statues of Gates, Schuyler, and Morgan. On the fourth side the niche for the hero of Saratoga is empty.

I especially wanted my children to see the second monument on that old battlefield. Much smaller than the obelisk is a statue of a leg, the leg of Benedict Arnold. In the evening of the battle of Saratoga, a wounded Hessian, lying on the ground, fired at

Arnold, shattering his left leg—that same leg that had been wounded at Quebec.

A rifleman, seeing the incident, rushed upon the Hessian with drawn bayonet. He was stopped only by Arnold's cry, "For God's sake, don't hurt him!" It has been well said that this was the hour when the brilliant young general should have died.

A few months later we find Benedict Arnold plotting with the British for the fall of West Point—a fort that Arnold was supposed to be commanding! By a chance coincidence, his plan was discovered, and he fled for his life to the British. The profit he received for his treachery was a few thousand dollars and a commission in the British army.

After becoming a Britisher, he asked an American prisoner, "What would the Americans do if they caught me?"

With contempt the American said, "They would cut off your wounded leg and give it the best of military burials. Then they would hang the rest of you."

Benedict Arnold started off well. He earned his reputation as one of early America's finest. But today his name does not remind us of brilliance, courage, or honor. Today he has no place of honor, either at Saratoga or in the hearts of his compatriots.

Benedict Arnold did not "hold true to what [he] had attained."

Editor Roy Adams asks in his editorial "Spiritual Alzheimer's" (*Adventist Review*, Oct. 1, 1992): "Could we come to the place where we feel . . . that the Adventist Church is too small for us, its standards too petty for us, its theology too narrow for us? Could the time come when, as individuals and as a people, we forget who we are [and] despise our heritage?

"The process by which a religious community forgets its identity does not happen overnight. Rather, it is gradual—brought on to a larger extent by social and intellectual absorption into the larger society. We succumb to the mood and spirit of a secular, pagan culture. We become defanged by it, domesticated by it, spiritually and emotionally confused by it. And we lose the sense of having something vital and urgent to say to it.

"Let's remember our roots, our heritage, our mission. To forget these is to forget who we are. To forget these is to succumb to spiritual Alzheimer's."

How many reading these pages can discuss for five minutes the immense significance of the year 1844? Or explain the basic factors in the cosmic controversy between God and Satan? Or remember the last time you prayed with your children, no matter how old? or with your spouse? or by yourself for more than 10 seconds?

Or express regret that the Sabbath should end so soon?

As that song pleads, "How long has it been . . . ?"

Of all people on earth, let us hold true to what we have attained. Let us remember, now and forever, that for Christians there is no finish line. Further, one of the most stress-free principles in life is learning how to keep the main thing the main thing. To know all this by experience is truly exciting—colossal reasons for joy!

Philippians 4:1-23

Living Without Anxiety

8

"If you will seek the Lord and be converted every day; if you will of your own spiritual choice be free and joyous in God; if with gladsome consent of heart to His gracious call you come wearing the yoke of Christ—the yoke of obedience and service—all your murmurings will be stilled, all your difficulties will be removed, all the perplexing problems that now confront you will be solved" *(Thoughts From the Mount of Blessing,* p. 101).

HERE again is a chapter (Phil. 4) that cries out for a book of its own. Let me trace down its high points, and you will see what I mean:

1. In verses 1-3 Paul gives us a peek into a vexing problem for pastors and church members since the first century—how to resolve squabbles, resentments, or outright hostilities among church members in "good and regular standing." His principles for reconciliation are profoundly simple—they work every time when people of good will are serious about agreeing "in the Lord."

2. In verses 4-7 we are listening to a veteran of many conflicts tell us the secret that undergirds his perseverance and optimism—how anxiety is turned to peace, no matter what!

3. In verses 8 and 9 Paul provides us with the elements of genuine success, the kind of mind nurturing that truly develops one's potential for maximum self-fulfillment and usefulness. On one side of the formula is the discipline of thinking healthful thoughts; the other side focuses on choosing the right heroes, the most helpful mentors—and copying their success habits.

4. Verses 10-13 contain some of the most quoted words in the entire Bible. Many books and sermons have done their best to spotlight the striking, memorable counsel Paul passes on from experience. Reading and rereading these verses is often comparable to returning again and again to an artesian well. These verses need no explanation, only a willingness to live out their truth; they contain a never-failing power and refreshment. Believe me, I know.

5. The promise in verse 19 should be posted on every bathroom mirror, on every car sun visor, on the flyleaf of every Bible, and should be included somewhere in every conversation with, or letter to, a burdened loved one or stranger. Try it and see!

Now you understand what I mean by a diverse but heavily freighted, divinely inspired chapter. All I can do in these few pages is simply point, and the reader will have to do the rest in mining the ore.

Take, for example, the apparently open, well-known conflict between Euodia and Syntyche. What would happen if the friction between you and the local elder in your church (hypothetical case, of course!) were so prominently revealed in the *Adventist Review*, or maybe in your pastor's church letter? Or what if the tension or conflict that keeps families, one-time friends, and even spouses cool to one another were to be exposed publicly?

Most of us know of situations in which church members haven't spoken to one another for years. Perhaps we notice some of these "hidden" currents more at nominating committee time. Perhaps many church members travel long distances to avoid attending their local church, or maybe they no longer attend any church—all because of the Euodia-Syntyche syndrome.

Obviously Euodia and Syntyche are prominent leaders in the church at Philippi. Perhaps both have many friends who tend to support one over the other. Perhaps both have outstanding, positive characteristics, and the local church needs both to "make things happen."

Perhaps they remind us of a Peanuts cartoon in which Lucy confronts Snoopy: "There are times when you really bug me, but I must admit there are also times when I feel like giving you a big hug."

Snoopy philosophically responds: "That's the way I am—huggable and buggable."

Do you know people like that in your family? in your neighborhood? of all places, in your church? Perhaps you are "huggable and buggable"! Where do we start to bring peace, lasting peace? (We are not referring to appropriate differences of opinion, or tastes, or personalities—those should be expected, part of God's gifts to each one of us. But we are focusing on such irritants as unnecessary nit-picking, power plays, verbal assaults, and misrepresentations.)

Let's look at Paul's tender yet compelling appeal. On what basis does he think any healing can begin?

First, he appeals to the larger picture in which all Christians should place themselves: "Stand firm thus in the Lord, my beloved" (Phil. 4:1). Later in this chapter Paul wants to say something very important about Christian joy—but he knows that his words will not be heard by those who don't find joy in their present strained relationships. Disharmony has a way of sapping joy in such a way that reason itself cannot prevail. Personal squabbles often loom up so big that words such as peace, love, and joy seem to have no meaning.

Why does Paul appeal to their "standing" with their Lord? Because no marital teamwork lasts for long without a mutual submission to our friendly Lord. Because no church grudge can be resolved if people do not first, and above all else, relate compliantly and joyfully with God. Paul has already written three incredible chapters spelling out what it means to have the mind of Jesus, to reflect His priorities, and to seek His will in all things. He now directs all this inspired counsel to a specific problem that must have been sufficiently weighty to require this public appeal!

Euodia and Syntyche (and their partisan supporters) were to ask themselves: "Am I standing with my friends, or my opinion—or am I standing firm with the Lord" (see Phil. 4:1)?

Notice that Paul does not rebuke them—he appeals to their conscience, to their Christian commitments. Nor does he command them to do something, or to follow three steps "that always work!" He simply uses a very strong Greek word as if he were pleading, "Please, Euodia, please, Syntyche, I beg you both to quarrel no more. Look at yourselves as Jesus looks at you. Think of how He has forgiven you time and time again. Adopt the same attitude, the same mind, toward each other, as Jesus has to each of you. Agree in the Lord!"

Then Paul suggests something further: these two women, who have both done so much for the building up of the church in Philippi, may need some kind objectivity. So he appeals to a highly respected church leader to "help these women" (verse 3). Not everyone is gifted in unprejudiced arbitration. Fortunate is the family or the church that has at least one.

After this bit of pastoral counsel, Paul pours himself into the most compact, most helpful prescription for living with stress found anywhere, in any language, it seems to me (verses 4-19). The secret of living with stress becomes also the formula for perseverance, optimism, and peace during tough times.

When most people think of stress, words such as anxiety, fear, despair, and failure come to mind. But stress can be positive or negative, depending upon the perception of the person. Stress, in a simple definition, is the response of the person (physically, mentally, and emotionally) to any kind of circumstance. Bungee jumping for me would be very *dis*-stressful; for an experienced daredevil, it would be sheer excitement and joy—that is, *un*-stress (good stress).

The same event, such as a B grade in classwork, can bring dis-stress or un-stress, depending on a student's point of view. If a student thought that not getting an A grade was a personal failure, then the B would be perceived as a destructive event. Another student may be very grateful for the B!

Paul may not have known all we know today about the physiological consequences of stress, including the profound interplay of mind and body during stress—but he surely knew the best response to stress from whatever source.

Read verses 4-13 carefully. Note words such as "rejoice," "always," "forbearance," "have no anxiety," "thanksgiving," "peace," "I am content," "learned the secret of facing plenty and hunger," "I can do all things in him who strengthens me."

I have a shelfful of books on managing stress. Through the years I have led out in stress clinics. The most helpful material that I have been able to pass on to those who are searching for steady ground in their lives has come out of Philippians 4. Many of the attendees at these clinics are burned-over church members who feel forgotten; many have no Christian ties—but they now understand the principles of Philippians 4.

We find here the open secret of joy, even during tough times. Joy is different than happiness. I find it more than interesting that God does not ask us to be happy, or to make others happy—for happiness depends too often on circumstances that shift with the wind, or on self-serving gratification. (After all, there is no happiness in being shipwrecked three times, receiving 39 lashes five times, being stoned, and suffering all kinds of dangers such as Paul experienced for at least 30 years as he served his Lord [see 2 Cor. 11:23-29]—but he knew how to rejoice in spite of it all.)

Rather, God does ask us to share the principles of joy. How does one do that? Perhaps you tell a burdened friend, "Buck up, rejoice, forbear, learn to be content." But is that all there is to it? What lies underneath these "right" words? Why is it, in your own life at times, that these words seem so distant, so foreign, to what you are really feeling?

Basic to experiencing our Christian privilege—to rejoice always, to be always content with whatever circumstance that we face—is the powerhouse of hope.

Hope is probably the most powerful of all human emotions. We all know what happens to people who feel they have no reason to hope!

A word that is very close to hope is optimism—which seems to be the more modern word for this compelling, driving emotion. The opposite of optimism is pessimism. But these words do get slippery. What do they mean?

For instance, some people believe they have hope for the return of Jesus, but they think and act pessimistically! And some others have no feeling for next year, never mind for an afterlife, yet they live optimistically: "You only live once; do it." "Life is a blast." "Live now."

Their approach is something like that of the man who is falling from a 10-story building. He waves to his friends on the fifth floor. "All right so far!" he says. That's being very optimistic, but without much hope. Some optimists, you might say, are not very realistic.

But then there was the man who had identical twin sons, one of whom was an optimist and the other a pessimist. He went to a psychiatrist for advice on how to handle them. The doctor told him that on Christmas morning he should fill the pessimist's room with toys and put only a pile of hay in the optimist's room.

The man complied. On Christmas morning the pessimist was found kicking his new bicycle because it was the wrong color. When the father asked the optimist what he had received for Christmas, this son replied, "I got a pony, but I haven't found it yet."

Do you know if you are an optimist or a pessimist? Try asking yourself, Do I give up easily? or Do I never seem to give up? Or think about two words: yes and no. These words lurk in everyone's deepest self, and one is most apt to be present when anything new or different happens. Are you a yes person or a no person—it's an almost unconscious response, and you probably never thought about it before. The answer to these questions will help you to understand why you may say the right words but have no joy—or it will affirm your confidence that Paul's formula for joy is working in your life.

It really does matter if you are an optimist or not. Research is abundant: optimists catch fewer infectious diseases than do pessimists; optimists have better health habits; the immune system works better for optimists; optimists live longer; optimists become the leaders of their groups; optimists find that people like to be around them.

Let's make this even more practical: right eating; vigorous exercise; wearing seat belts; avoiding alcohol, tobacco, sugar— all this together is a terrific lifestyle program. I have watched it for years while I was president of Weimar Institute—that remarkable international center for reversing atherosclerosis, hypertension, diabetes, and a host of other lifestyle-related diseases.

The full NEWSTART® package, which emphasizes the final T (trust in God) as much as the big N (nutrition) or E (exercise), is God's way to avoid much of life's physical problems. It also helps one to be a cheerful, joyful person. But not all NEW-START® guests make progress. Though these few exercised and maintained low cholesterol readings, they could not internalize such concepts as hope, trust, and optimism. Their problems were deeper than physical.

The best part of all is that no one needs to be pessimistic; no one needs to be demoralized by hopelessness. Optimism is a learned attitude. We can unlearn pessimistic habits. These are some of the most important facts that psychologists have confirmed in the past 20 years.

Optimism is not a new way to describe "the power of positive thinking." We have found that saying positive things to ourselves and others has little or no lasting effect. What is important is *what we think* when we fail, or when unpleasant events happen—events that we all experience, probably every day.

If we wanted a label for this mental phenomenon, it could be "the power of non-negative thinking." How do we change the destructive things we say to ourselves when we experience setbacks? That is the skill that realistic optimists have learned, either by observing other optimists (note Paul's counsel in Philippians 4:9: "What you have learned and received and heard and seen in me, do") or by going through the process of changing their opinions about what is happening (the way we think: "Think about these things" [verse 8]).

By definition, optimists are not prone to depression. An optimist may have the same life setbacks as a pessimist—but he chooses to think differently about them. (Remember, stressors may be positive or negative, depending on a person's subjective response.)

We all know what momentary helplessness is—when we say the wrong thing, we damage our car, our investments go sour, people let us down, we miss an appointment. Or we may be more familiar with more lasting helplessness when we slip back into the old way of living that brought on our diabetes, our hypertension, our bronchial problems, or our internal habit of immediately saying No to the new and different. Full-blown helplessness shoots right past pessimism into depression.

This depression may be temporary, or it may be more long-lasting. But it all depends on how we explain to ourselves and others the reality (the truth) of these setbacks, how they really happened, and how we will optimistically perceive them.

I feel the need to reemphasize that pessimism can be unlearned. Pessimism is a strong risk factor for physical disease and mental/emotional depression, just as surely as smoking is a risk factor for lung cancer. Pessimists think that (1) whatever is happening is nonchangeable ("I'm just like my mother—I'll always be this way!"); (2) everything he or she does is no good ("I'm not good at anything!"); or (3) somehow it's always his or her fault ("I'm just not strong enough!" "I'm not as smart as other people!").

So you see, for a pessimist who may be bound for depression, everything seems to be permanent, pervasive, and personal. (For more specific help in changing minds and lives from pessimism to optimism, I highly recommend Martin Seligman's *Learned Optimism* [New York: Pocket Books, 1990], to whom I am indebted for enriching this chapter.)

Two thousand years ago Paul was teaching us how to live optimistically, joyfully, in the real world, where surprises, disappointments, failures, interruptions, and downright disloyalty of trusted friends are *part of everyone's life*—even more, perhaps, for those who set their sails to follow their friendly Master. "For the sake of Christ you should not only believe in him but also suffer for his sake, engaged in the same conflict which you saw and now hear to be mine" (Phil. 1:29, 30).

By God's enabling grace, Christians may learn how to be joyful and optimistic. They make it a life pattern to say: "I have learned, in whatever state I am, to be content. . . . I can do all things in him who strengthens me" (Phil. 4:11-13).

Alexandr Solzhenitsyn tells of his Russian gulag experience—he was a political prisoner for years. For long periods of time, the prisoners were not even allowed to speak. Further, they were forbidden to read.

Solzhenitsyn said that the strain and repression became overwhelming. He thought, *I will never get out of here.* So he planned how he would end his life. He knew that if he tried to escape, he would be shot—"and that will be the end of that."

The next day, as usual, he was taken with the rest of the prisoners out to work. When a break came, he sat under a tree. He even placed his hand against the tree, ready to push off and run. Just then a shadow came across the grass. A fellow prisoner sat down beside him. Although forbidden to speak, he could at least look into the eyes of the other prisoner. He saw something he had rarely seen in any face before—a message of love and concern.

As their eyes locked in silence, they started communicating in their souls. The other prisoner took a step forward and with a stick in his hand drew a cross in the sand.

Solzhenitsyn felt new hope surge within him. He remembers his thoughts—*God has not forsaken me. He loves me. He is still in charge. There is still hope!* He would live on! And so he did. He has become one of the greatest writers and motivators of the twentieth century.

The power of thinking straight, of rejoicing in hope, in learning how to be content—all that is the Christian's privilege! Hope is fantastic power that builds on the proven promises of God, on something so simple as a cross in the sand! Nothing is so desperate as the death of hope—here is where the laserlike clearness and power of Philippians 4 can make the difference.

No wonder Paul ended this chapter with these words, confirmed day after day in his own life: "My God will supply every need of yours according to his riches in glory in Christ Jesus" (Phil. 4:19).

The compelling dynamics behind joy is Christian hope—a realistic, quiet trust in the realistic promises of the gospel. We are "saved by hope" (Rom. 8:24, KJV).

Letting God Qualify Us

9

"The manifestation of real goodness is the bearing of fruit in good works. This bears the endorsement of heaven. Read the first chapter of Paul's Epistle to the Colossians. The instruction it contains is of the highest value. The religion of Christ makes all who possess it truly benevolent. It countenances no littleness, no mean transactions. True Christians have a nobility which allows none of the cheap, covetous actions that are a disgrace to the doer of them" *(SDA Bible Commentary,* Ellen G. White Comments, vol. 7, pp. 905, 906).

I AM having difficulty confining what I want to say within the space limitations for each chapter in this book. I can't even tell you which chapter has given me the most joy to write. Each one has been a remarkable experience for me, not only to present concisely what I think must be said, but to share to some degree the joyful elation I have experienced with each chapter.

However, the first chapter of Colossians surely stands by itself in its majestic sweep of several towering subjects: (1) Paul's use of the awesome triad—faith, love, and hope (Col. 1:4, 5); (2) his description of the purpose of the gospel (verses 6, 10-12, 21-23); and (3) his wonderful delineation of the person and work of Jesus (verses 15-21). All this is more than we can fully grasp—even if we had unlimited publishing capabilities!

We will be emphasizing some of these subjects in other chapters. But for now let us look briefly at the triad and then Paul's clear-cut picture of the purpose of the gospel and how this purpose is achieved.

Faith, love, and hope—which is greater? Careful now! In a way, each of them expresses the whole experience of the Christian life.

I first saw the interrelationship of these three basic Christian experiences when I read Emil Brunner's Earl Lectures, given at the Pacific School of Religion in 1955. He described how we all live in three dimensions of time at once—the past, in memory; the present, where we make our decisions; and the future, by expectation, whether in hope or fear.

In the New Testament we learn how our relationship to Jesus directly affects how we look at the past, the present, and the future. We live in the past by faith, the present by love, and the future by hope.

When Paul speaks of "your faith in Christ Jesus" (verse 4), he is distinguishing Christianity from all other religions of the world. In Christianity, God became man at a specific time in history. He lived and died in the full glare of human observation. He was buried in a tomb, as any dead person would be cared for. More than that, He was resurrected and ascended to heaven. His words and acts were recorded and reaffirmed by eyewitnesses. No one questioned the facts of His remarkable life, death, and resurrection.

Faith is built on that kind of rock-bottom historicity. No reason to doubt the basis of Christianity—it is a fact. A convincing fact! Enough to send the early Christians throughout the then-known world (Rom. 1:8) at great personal risk; for this gospel most of them were terribly persecuted and many murdered. God has spoken in the Man Jesus Christ. He is not only God who speaks; He also loves and offers forgiveness and grace to rescue us from our human predicament. These are facts! The Christian's total response to these facts is called *faith*.

Love is the way by which God changes our present. The Christian's faith responds to the God of love revealed in the historical Jesus and believes His promises. Believing in and responding to the God of such love changes the believer. (We are not talking about the many perversions of our English word "love." We certainly do not think of New Testament love in the same context as "making love," nor with the same meaning as to love fresh peaches or a beautiful sunset.)

Love, as defined by our friendly God's actions to this rebel world, is a reaching out to others without selfish motivation—a giving and not a getting as our primary motivation. This kind of love, even toward strangers, even toward one's enemies, can be awakened and nurtured only by the grace of God. And that is Paul's point in many of his letters.

Christian love is what we are to do between the past and the future. Faith and hope, informed by the gospel, make the present more meaningful and more enjoyable, awakening us to our highest and best moments—the loving opportunities of the present. I know that it is difficult to think of the present, because as soon as we do, it has already become past. In the same way, the future has already become present. But we still understand what we mean by the "present"—the time when we make choices, when we take advantage of *the moment*. During these moments we think and act—during this present time Christians are to make loving thoughts and loving acts.

The problem is that too many of us have not really related to the past as God wants us to. Too often we carry the burden of the past, the guilt, the missed or misused opportunities, forgetting that Jesus has promised to carry your past, your guilt, your regrets, and to cast them as far away as the east is from the west. Believe it! Your faith is based on a historical Person who has demonstrated His ability to do such wonderful things! This release from the clutching fingers of the past liberates us to love more freely, more spontaneously, more joyfully. Ah, there's that word again—joy!

But now *hope*—this is the way we live in the future! That is, if we really have faith, then we live in the future with hope. Little faith, little hope! Too many people look at the future in fear, or with apprehension or anxiety. Hope is the opposite of fear. Hope is based on knowledge that only a Christian has—knowledge that arises from within his faith. Remember chapter 7!

The Bible is very clear about what God has on His mind regarding the future. This world will not end in a bang or a whimper—but in a glorious happening. Jesus, with His heavenly entourage, will usher in eternity for His redeemed. Just as surely as Jesus ascended to heaven, so will He return "in the same way as you saw him go into heaven" (Acts 1:11).

Truly, without a clear understanding about the return of Jesus and the nature of life after death, either for the redeemed or the unsaved, no one on earth can offer anyone any concrete reason for hope for the future. As we saw in chapter 7, hope is to the human spirit what oxygen is to our lungs—and we all need hope as well as breath as we lean into the future, if we expect to go without fear or anxiety.

As Emil Brunner put it: "Faith believes what hope expects. Hope expects what faith believes. But both faith and hope have their real content in the love of God revealed in Christ. . . . Faith and hope are about God, about the God of love, about God's love. Therefore they are nothing in themselves; they are something only by their relation to love. That is why Saint Paul says that the greatest among them is love. Not the most important— they are equally important. . . . But love is the real substance of faith and hope" (*Faith, Hope, and Love* [Philadelphia: Westminster Press, 1956], p. 77).

Only the Christian who lives in faith and hope is free to really love. And only those who can love freely and spontaneously will have real joy. Call it peace, love, or joy—they seem to go together. Only those who have faith and hope and thus love can live above the uncertainties and troubles of life. They even live triumphantly above the dark valley of death—that is joy in its highest form.

Now the next major theme in Colossians 1: how God works to prepare His redeemed for eternal life. In chapter 3 we focused on the "harvest principle." We reviewed how Biblical writers used this principle to describe the planting of the gospel seed in those who make Jesus their Lord. We noted that this first chapter of Colossians focused on how the gospel was already "bearing fruit and growing" (Col. 1:6), that the purpose of the gospel is to assist people "to lead a life worthy of the Lord, fully pleasing to him, bearing fruit in every good work and increasing in the knowledge of God" (verse 10).

Next Paul describes how this salvation plan works: "May you be strengthened with all power, according to his glorious might, for all endurance and patience with joy, giving thanks to the

Father, who has qualified us to share in the inheritance of the saints in light" (verses 11, 12).

These texts are among the most overlooked texts in the Bible! Rarely do we hear sermons on these remarkable, inspiring words of great peace and hope. In chapter 6 we emphasized the awesome formula of salvation: our will + God's grace = overcoming lives, or salvation. Here in verse 11 we again see how God's grace works—what His "glorious might" does for us. He strengthens us to endure, to face life with joy regardless of earthly circumstances—to become part of the wonderful group who "endure," as described in Revelation 14:12.

But something further in verse 12 ties together many other biblical texts: God is the "qualifier" of those who are safe to save. We sense again the meaning of Philippians 2:13: "For God is at work in you, both to will and to work for his good pleasure."

I think you hear Paul's salvation formula and God's qualifying work in that glorious picture of the redeemed in Revelation 19: "Then I heard what seemed to be the voice of a great multitude, like the sound of many waters and like the sound of mighty thunderpeals, crying, 'Hallelujah! For the Lord our God the Almighty reigns. Let us rejoice and exult and give him the glory, for the marriage of the Lamb has come, and his Bride has made herself ready; it was granted her to be clothed with fine linen, bright and pure'—for the fine linen is the righteous deeds of the saints" (verses 6-8).

The first part of the formula reads: "His Bride has made herself ready. . . . The fine linen is the righteous deeds of the saints." The second part is: "Give him the glory . . . ; it was granted [given] her to be clothed with fine linen."

The Bible is not a book of paradoxes or dilemmas or genuine antinomies—as we hear so often these days. When one understands the issues involved in the great controversy, especially regarding how sin is removed from a person's life so that he or she is safe to save—the Bible is a beautiful unfolding of a common theme. That theme is Paul's salvation formula: our will + God's grace = overcomers (or our salvation).

Jesus depicted this formula in His parable of the wedding

garment (Matt. 22:1-14). We are told that this "parable . . . opens before us a lesson of the highest consequence. By the marriage is represented the union of humanity with divinity; the wedding garment represents the character which all must possess who shall be accounted fit guests for the wedding" (*Christ's Object Lessons*, p. 307).

Recognize our formula? "Union of humanity with divinity." The result of this formula is more powerful than $E = mc^2$: "character . . . fit . . . for the wedding." Could we ever hope for any more than that!

How does this parable explain further the secret of this formula? Three calls to the wedding are given: (1) that given by Christ and His disciples before the cross (verses 2, 3); (2) that given to the Jewish nation after Christ's crucifixion to those who should have been the most prepared for the fulfillment of their own Scriptures (verses 4-7); (3) that given to the Gentiles as well as to seeking Jews (verses 8-10).

The parable gets very instructive: "The king came in to look at the guests [and] saw there a man who had no wedding garment" (verse 11).

"When the king came in to view the guests, the real character of all was revealed. For every guest at the feast there had been provided a wedding garment. This garment was a gift from the king" (*ibid.*, p. 309).

The king's simple question revealed the awful truth: "How did you expect to attend the wedding without the wedding garment I had made available to you?"

Because the guest tried to gain entrance without fulfilling his part in preparing himself with the king's own gift, he was self-condemned—"He was speechless" (verse 12)! The salvation formula works only when all factors are operating together. Grace does not fulfill its intention if faith does not cooperate with it. Without the cooperation of faith with grace, there is no salvation.

But let's look further into the lessons contained in this parable. "The guests at the gospel feast are those who profess to serve God, those whose names are written in the book of life. But not all who profess to be Christians are true disciples. Before the final reward is given, it must be decided who are fitted to share the inheritance of the righteous. This decision must be made prior to the second coming of Christ. . . . Before His coming, then, the character of every man's work will have been determined, and to every one of Christ's followers the reward will have been apportioned according to his deeds" (*ibid.*, p. 310).

Here again we see the clear message (as we did in chapter 6): our eternal destiny is determined by the life record *before Jesus comes*. "It is in this life that we are to put on the robe of Christ's righteousness. This is our opportunity to form characters for the home which Christ has made ready for those who obey His commandments" (*ibid.*, p. 319; see *Testimonies*, vol. 1, p. 705; vol. 2, pp. 355, 356; *Testimonies to Ministers*, p. 430; *Signs of the Times*, Sept. 29, 1887).

Adventists today need to settle this biblical principle. Too much Calvinistic evangelicalism has permeated our thinking during the past 30 years. Various forms of Calvinism are in tension within Evangelical Protestantism—they range from (1) the summary statement that overcoming sin is not only impossible but also unnecessary in the salvation process to (2) the Lordship faction, which believes that sanctification is possible and necessary—but only to be enjoyed by the "elect." Seepage from these differing groups must be constantly guarded against.

Perhaps one more carefully worded statement may help us to see the longstanding, basic Adventist position on how our characters affect our destiny: "If you would be a saint in heaven you must first be a saint on earth. The traits of character you cherish in life will not be changed by death or by the resurrection. You will come up from the grave with the same disposition you manifested in your home and in society. Jesus does not change the character at His coming. The work of transformation must be done now. Our daily lives are determining our destiny. Defects of character must be repented of and overcome through the grace of Christ, and a symmetrical character must be formed while in this probationary state, that we may be fitted for the mansions above" (*Last Day Events*, p. 295).

But how does this really work? How can I be assured that

what Jesus begins, He will finish (remember chapter 3!)? How can I see this formula work in my life? In other words, "What must I do to be saved?"

The wedding parable speaks to this point. For instance, let's be clear as to what is meant by the "wedding garment" that we all must "possess" so that we may be "fitted for the mansions above."

"By the wedding garment in the parable is represented the pure, spotless character which Christ's true followers will possess. To the church is given 'that she should be arrayed in fine linen, clean and white.'. . . The fine linen, says the Scripture, 'is the righteousness of saints' (Eph. 5:27). It is the righteousness of Christ, His own unblemished character, that through faith is imparted to all who receive Him as their personal Saviour" (*Christ's Object Lessons*, p. 310).

Here again is the formula of salvation: receive Jesus as personal Saviour + character imparted = character—wedding garment. Let's examine how we receive and "possess" the "imparted" fine linen, or character.

The following words are very helpful: "When we submit ourselves to Christ, the heart is united with His heart, the will is merged in His will, the mind becomes one with His mind, the thoughts are brought into captivity to Him; we live His life. This is what it means to be clothed with the garment of His righteousness" (*ibid.*, p. 312).

Notice the verbs in those two sentences: submit, unite, merge, become, live, clothed. These are powerful action words. Nothing passive about these verbs. They sound like the words emphasized in chapter 6: strive, abide, resist, etc.

Another question that arises often is What does "righteousness" mean? I have been told by many in the past 20 years that righteousness is something done light-years away for me by Christ, in virtue of what He did for me on the cross! Period!

That is partly true, but anything partly true fabricates a total error. Whatever else we want, nothing is more important than being "clothed with the garment of His righteousness." Some in Christian thought, both in Catholicism and Protestantism, think primarily in terms of "imputed" righteousness; others overly stress "imparted" righteousness. I wish that the quarreling theologians who emphasize one of these aspects of "righteousness" over the other would go off to Mars and there discuss their mental constructs—and false emphases—and let the common people just read the Bible from Genesis to Revelation for the whole story.

I like the succinctness of this definition: "Righteousness is right doing, and it is by their deeds that all will be judged. Our characters are revealed by what we do. The works show whether the faith is genuine. . . . Whatever our profession, it amounts to nothing unless Christ is revealed in works of righteousness" (*ibid.*, pp. 312, 313).

This definition fits anyone who prefers to use the English words "imputed" and "imparted." In the wedding parable, as anywhere else in the Bible, the attitude of repentance and submission to Christ's free grace (which is the experience that makes justification effective), the yearning to desire what His heart desires, the honest compliance of will to do His will, the submission of thoughts to what He wants us to think—all this is living the life of a genuine disciple. This "right" relationship between God and His disciples covers the whole experience from the awakening awareness of His love for us (that draws us quietly to Him— Rom. 2:4) to the "completeness of Christian character," wherein "the impulse to help and bless others springs constantly from within" (*ibid.*, p. 384).

Thus, righteousness imputed and righteousness imparted (terms not found as such in the Bible) describe how God draws us to Himself (He includes everyone—Titus 2:11); how He blankets us with His forgiveness for our sins, past and present; and how He empowers us with His Spirit ("by the washing of rebirth and renewal" [Titus 3:7]) to live out Christ's life as a daily choice and walk—if we choose to respond to His overtures!

In theological terms, justification (righteousness imputed) and sanctification (righteousness imparted) are both fruits of the Holy Spirit. Neither could happen without the prompting, enabling, friendly Spirit. Likewise, neither could happen without the Christian's willing repentance and submission, without his or her earnest compliance, without his or her single-eyed commitment to will to do God's will.

One of the most helpful thoughts I have found linking imputed and imparted righteousness is on page 63 of *Steps to Christ:* "Our only ground of hope is in the righteousness of Christ imputed to us, and in that wrought by His Spirit working in and through us." We must not, in any fashion, "break asunder what God hath joined together."

Whenever you see or hear the word "righteousness," think of God's declaration that you are always His child whom He wants to make His obedient friend; His onetime little rebel whom He turns into His loyal representative. Then immediately think of what He has promised to do in you and for you, from the first moment you burst out your guilt and claimed His forgiveness all the way to that time when He believes you "qualified . . . to share in the inheritance of the saints in light" (Col. 1:12).

One caution: in an important sense we are "qualified" for God's kingdom as soon as we honestly, wholeheartedly, claim Jesus as our Lord and our Saviour. Think of the thief on the cross: the gospel seed was planted in his heart when he capitulated to the Holy Spirit's prompting that Jesus was Lord. For however long he lived, that seed kept growing. In that sense, every Christian should remain in joyful awareness that God will qualify us for His kingdom. For how long? As long as we choose to continue permitting the Holy Spirit to nurture, "to grow," the gospel principles into our neural paths—whether we live two hours or 100 years after our initial conversion experience.

The principle remains: Only those who continue to submit to Jesus as Lord, who continue to merge their will with His will, who consciously choose to live His life in their daily thoughts and actions, are those who can enjoy the joy and "peace of God, which passes all understanding" (Phil. 4:7).

Mistakes, yes, perhaps grievous sins we will commit in this growth period. But the joy of salvation accompanies the heart remorse for these weaknesses—and even deliberate self-indulgences. How quickly we should throw ourselves on the friendly Rock that breaks up our sinful patterns! (Note David's longing expressed in Psalm 51 for the joy he lost because of his deliberate sin: "Restore to me the joy of thy salvation, and uphold me with a willing spirit" [verse 12]). If David did not have that deep repentance described in Psalm 51, he surely would not have been God's friend—he would not have been a "saved" man, as so many have proclaimed during the past 30 years!

In those dark moments that we have shared at times with David, remember, nothing can take us out of our friendly Father's arms except our own perverse willfulness, our stubborn pride! Our loving heavenly Friend always seems to be standing in the road, with arms outstretched, waiting for His wayward sons and daughters to return home.

Keep the following promise close to your heart: "In every command or injunction that God gives there is a promise, the most positive, underlying the command. God has made provision that we may become like unto Him, and He will accomplish this for all who do not interpose a perverse will and thus frustrate His grace" (*Thoughts From the Mount of Blessing*, p. 76).

But Satan and many others have said that all the above is pure salvation by works, that it is impossible for sinful human beings to be true overcomers this side of the resurrection. To try to "keep the law" is pure legalism, they say! (See chapter 12 for further thoughts on legalism.)

Well, which is right, Satan's point of view, or God's simple declarations in the Bible and in the writings of His modern messenger?

Listen to His messenger: "Satan had claimed that it was impossible for man to obey God's commandments; and in our own strength it is true that we cannot obey them. But Christ came in the form of humanity, and by His perfect obedience He proved that humanity and divinity combined [our salvation formula] can obey every one of God's precepts. . . . When a soul receives Christ, he receives power to live the life of Christ" (*Christ's Object Lessons*, p. 314).

Our friendly Lord is waiting for "qualified" people through whom one day soon He will give the power of the Holy Spirit to finish the worldwide proclamation of the gospel. The methods He will help His people use will surprise us all. But He will not embarrass His honor or His name by giving His power to people who will misrepresent Him and the truth. He is looking for "qualified" people!

He does not want us to make any "mistake in regard to the kind of people whom God will have to compose His kingdom. The life of Christ on earth was a perfect expression of God's law, and when those who claim to be children of God become Christlike in character, they will be obedient to God's commandments. Then the Lord can trust them to be of the number who shall compose the family of heaven. . . . They have a right to join the blood-washed throng" (*ibid*., p. 315).

Let us return to the wedding parable and God's gift that qualifies His guests: *the gift includes what God does for us and what He does in and through us.* This two-phased gift cannot be separated any more than the two sides of a pane of glass can be separated. And again the caution: "Those who reject the gift of Christ's righteousness are rejecting the attributes of character which would constitute them the sons and daughters of God. They are rejecting that which alone could give them a fitness for a place at the marriage feast" (*ibid.*, pp. 316, 317).

Could you think of a better offer, not only for the next world, but also for our life today? Truly God is speaking to us all through our Lord's wedding parable—the story that colors in the expansive picture of Paul's challenge in Colossians 1.

Knowing the Secret of the Mystery

10

"Pure and undefiled religion is not a sentiment, but the doing of works of mercy and love. This religion is necessary to health and happiness. It enters the polluted soul-temple, and with a scourge drives out the sinful intruders. Taking the throne, it consecrates all by its presence, illuminating the heart with the bright beams of the Sun of Righteousness. It opens the windows of the soul heavenward, letting in the sunshine of God's love. With it comes serenity and composure. Physical, mental, and moral strength increase, because the atmosphere of heaven, as a living, active agency, fills the soul. Christ is formed within, the hope of glory" *(Review and Herald,* Oct. 15, 1901).

WE LIVE in a world possessed by "mysteries." Scholarly circles call it parapsychology, or paranormal activity. Gallup polls indicate that 80 percent of Americans "read" their future in the daily astrology columns; even a U.S. president's wife took seriously the counsel of her astrologist in arranging her husband's schedule.

UFO sightings, channeling, interplanetary communications, global harmonics, quartz pyramids, "the other side," transmigration (reincarnation), occult phenomena—all these terms and many similar ones have become common vocabulary in the past 30 years.

Among the most-watched movies of all time are the *Star Wars* trilogy wherein Luke Skywalker gets the victory every time because he relies on "the force." I first learned about "the force" when I overheard young people in a news broadcast tell each other as they said their daily goodbyes: "May the force be with you!" The problem with these young people is that the line between fact and fiction is blurred—that somehow, they think, this interspace activity is all possible eventually! Further, the force to them has supplanted our heavenly Creator and Friend—the genuine force of the universe!

We include all this recent emphasis on finding "meaning in feeling," in reaching for security in "spiritual" forces, and employing intuition to guide decision-making under the umbrella term the New Age movement. Not easily defined, the central thread is the subjective search for peace, harmony, and direction. New Agers look within for the feeling of divinity, or to Eastern religions for age-old philosophical frameworks. One thing that identifies most New Agers, it seems to me, is that they are not looking for, or attempting to listen to, a personal God. Strange as it may seem, some New Agers call themselves Christians, not realizing that much of their thinking is cross-grained with biblical truths. Most New Agers who once were Christians have now moved on to "spirits," "self-understanding," and "self-actualization" for peace and security. Their end is dismal to contemplate.

The tragedy of this modern drama is that the Bible, of all books, talks about mysteries that the world should be excited about. Paul thought he knew religion until he met Jesus on the Damascus Road. But the story of Jesus, the crucified carpenter, was a remarkable mystery that had to be told. This Man, whose hometown was Nazareth, was God—truly an interplanetary, intergalactic traveler. And He truly had much to say about the "other side." That was heavy stuff for first-century Jews and Gentiles!

In Romans 16:25-27 Paul wrote that the purpose of "the mystery which was kept secret for long ages" was to "bring about the obedience of faith." In 1 Timothy 3:16 Paul notes that the elements of the gospel are truly a mystery to those who only look within—to human reason, to historical research, to intuition, to feeling—for truth.

Now, in Colossians 1:25-27 Paul speaks bluntly: the purpose of preaching, the preacher's primary task, is to "make the word of God fully known, the mystery hidden for ages and generations but now made manifest to his saints. To them God chose to make known how great among the Gentiles are the riches of the glory of this mystery, which is Christ in you, the hope of glory."

This is straight talk to preachers! What is the preacher's highest concern when he enters the pulpit? How would a congregation know if their preacher understands the gospel? Litmus test: Does he bring us the hope of the gospel—the tremendous good news that Christ (in some way that may be beyond full understanding) will live within us to make a difference in our lives? Bottom line: We don't have to get what we deserve! We don't have to be what we are!

This is marvelously good news! As we have been discussing in previous chapters, God has made provision whereby we may truly overcome our inherited and cultivated tendencies to sin. Sin keeps us from bringing glory to God—and bringing glory to God is the purpose for the existence of God's people.

It's a mystery to the worldly-minded how "men and women have broken the chains of sinful habit. They have renounced selfishness. The profane have become reverent, the drunken sober, the profligate pure. Souls that have borne the likeness of Satan, have been transformed into the image of God. The change wrought by the Word, it is one of the deepest mysteries of the Word. We can not understand it; we can only believe, that as declared by the Scriptures, it is 'Christ in you, the hope of glory'" (*Signs of the Times*, April 25, 1906).

Just let Paul's words sink in—"Christ in you, the hope of glory." Dwell on them for a few minutes. The Creator of the universe has promised, in some way that I can't fully understand, to live in our minds, to direct our thoughts, to steer our actions, "to bring about the obedience of faith" (Rom. 16:26).

I know you are thinking: *That sounds wonderful! I've heard it before—but somehow I don't get "the hang" of it! It sounds too romantic, too fuzzy. Somehow, it doesn't seem to really work, no matter how many times I sing "Into my heart, into my heart, Come into my heart, Lord Jesus."*

How can this experience really happen in my life, someone is asking. Let's review six rock-solid steps whereby Paul's promise becomes a living reality in our lives.

Step 1: Recognize that our friendly Lord is waiting to set up an internal relationship with you ("I stand at the door and knock" [Rev. 3:20]). Our response should be obvious: "Please, Lord, come in, right now!" (Caution! To receive Christ is not to hope for a gushing, warm feeling as a test that He is indeed within us!)

Step 2: Listen to His personal word to us in the Bible. Please don't treat the following paragraphs lightly, either by saying "Oh, I've read that before" or "That sounds like too much effort." Believe me, this second step is the surest way to find personal stamina, quiet assurance, and an anxiety-free look into the future. Use your yellow marker, red pencil, or whatever you have, and mark the thoughts in the next few paragraphs that are fresh for you.

First, from the Bible: "Unless you eat the flesh of the Son of man and drink his blood, you have no life in you. . . . He who eats my flesh and drinks my blood abides in me, and I in him" (John 6:53-56).

Now from my favorite author: "To eat the flesh and drink the blood of Christ is to receive Him as a personal Saviour, believing that He forgives our sins, and that we are complete in Him. . . . A theoretical knowledge will do us no good. We must feed upon Him, receive Him into the heart, so that His life becomes our life. . . .

"The life of Christ that gives life to the world is in His word. . . . The whole Bible is a manifestation of Christ, and the Saviour desired to fix the faith of His followers on the word. When His visible presence should be withdrawn, the word must be their source of power. Like their Master, they are to live 'by every word that proceedeth out of the mouth of God' (Matt. 4:4, KJV). . . .

"As we must eat for ourselves in order to receive nourishment, so we must receive the word for ourselves. We are not to obtain it merely through the medium of another's mind. We should carefully study the Bible, asking God for the aid of the Holy Spirit, that we may understand His word. . . .

"As faith thus receives and assimilates the principles of truth, they become a part of the being and the motive power of the life. The word of God, received into the soul, molds the thoughts, and enters into the development of character" (*The Desire of Ages*, pp. 389-391).

Is that test too much? Do you indeed want the grace, patience, kindness, and self-sacrificing love of Jesus? For those who first listened to our Lord's word in Galilee, many lost their interest in Him. Why? They wanted His miracles, the earthly rewards, the freedom from disease and suffering; "but they would not come into sympathy with His self-sacrificing life" (*The Desire of Ages*, p. 391).

As we hasten to the third step in making "Christ in you" a joyful reality, let's notice another caution light! Too many earnest seekers start well, even enthusiastically—but their interest soon wanes. With gusto they begin, often on January 1: "Now I know what I should do—I shall read my Bible more faithfully, I will act as Jesus would act. I will read three chapters daily and five on Sabbath!" But the days grow long, somehow even dreary, in this determined effort to make "Christ in me" a reality.

They need to understand step 3: Let God work!

Listen to Isaiah's promise: "For as the rain and the snow come down from heaven, and return not thither but water the earth, making it bring forth and sprout, giving seed to the sower and bread to the eater, so shall my word be that goes forth from my mouth; it shall not return to me empty, but it shall accomplish that which I purpose, and prosper in the thing for which I sent it" (Isa. 55:10, 11).

What does this mean? Does the farmer work harder in order to make the rain do its work on his seeds? Hardly! The most the farmer can do after he plants his seeds is to pull the weeds that would choke the growth of the seed. But the growth of the seed is not the result of the farmer's determination; growth happens by the mysterious action of the rain and sun.

Isaiah tells us, along with many other biblical writers, that the rain and snow accomplish their work as God purposes, not as the farmer purposes—because there is nothing that the farmer can do except to "let it happen" after he has done his part. As the farmer's part is to sow the seed, so the Christian's part is to study the Word.

God's part is reflected clearly in 1 Thessalonians 2:13: "For this reason we also thank God without ceasing, because when you received the word of God which you heard from us, you welcomed it not as the word of men, but as it is in truth, the word of God, which also effectively works in you who believe" (NKJV).

In Colossians 2 Paul finishes his emphasis on the open mystery: "Christ in you, the hope of glory. . . . Him we preach. . . . To this end I also labor, striving according to His working which works in me mightily" (verses 27-29, NKJV).

Let God work! Let the rain fall. Keep planting the seed—and trust God to water it. His Word is more than the letters on the page of your Bible. His Word spoke worlds into existence (Ps. 33:6, 9); His Word drove demons away (Matt. 8:32) and raised Lazarus (John 11:43). His Word creates—whether new worlds or new men and women. And He is very good at what He does.

I can't explain this power; it's a mystery. But the evidence of what happens when God speaks is everywhere. Note Paul's jubilation: "I am not ashamed of the gospel: it is the power of God for salvation to everyone who has faith" (Rom. 1:16).

I know you are asking yourself, "Is that all? Just let God do it?" Yes and no, as we saw in chapter 6.

We can't do God's part—and He will not do our part!

Thus, step 4 (All the steps work simultaneously, although logically we are forced to list them in sequence because we can't say everything in the same breath!): Trust and obey. Our response to God's initiative and to the growing seeds of truth that He has promised to water is called "faith" in the Bible—a word that has been more abused than any other, except perhaps for the word *grace*, during 2,000 years of Christian thought. (In the next chapter we will focus on the New Testament meaning of faith.)

For now, let us think of faith as being that heartfelt response of appreciation, repentance, and trusting obedience, to those growing seeds of truth about God.

Step 5: Focus on "glory" in the phrase "Christ in you, the hope of glory." We discussed in chapter 3 the special responsibility that rests on those who sense the assignment given to God's people in Revelation 14. The message of the first angel identifies and defines the message the world is to hear in the last days: "Fear God and give him glory, for the hour of his judgment has come" (Rev. 14:7).

We noted in chapter 3 that "to give glory to God is to reveal His character in our own, and thus make Him known" (*SDA Bible Commentary*, Ellen G. White Comments, vol. 7, p. 979). In our understanding of this privilege—"giving glory to God"—lies the rock-bottom support for lasting joy.

Step 5 gives focus to our lives: Do we live to impress God or to honor Him? To honor Him is to glorify Him.

I understand well the bewilderment: How can weak, self-oriented human beings glorify God? We don't have the willpower, even if our motives were pure. We couldn't do it regardless of how many self-help books we read—at least, not for long. The glaring dark hole of honest despair sets in sooner or later. Without the supernatural help of humanity's Best Friend, no one can rise above self-interest. In other words, without "Christ in you," no hope, no glory, no joy.

We must not think of these biblical words—joy, hope, glory, and fruits of righteousness (all powerful Pauline words)—as merely poetical, metaphorical terms. Experiencing these words or not experiencing them directly affects our physical health, our mental clarity, and our emotional stability—and thus our spiritual health. In a very real way, these great words shine as facets of the same diamond. They all belong to the men and women of faith, those who are "in Christ" and those whom Christ is "in."

Whatever hope we may have of glorifying God in the time of His judgment, whatever hope we may have of "possessing" the wedding garment (chapter 9), whatever hope we may have of Paul's salvation formula working in our lives (chapter 6)—depends on listening closely to Paul's clear warning in this section of the Colossian letter.

He had contemporaries, his preaching colleagues, who were preaching a message that sounds much like what we call "cheap grace" today. We see the same concern in Romans, Galatians, and other Pauline letters. After stating clearly that the mystery of the gospel is "Christ in you," that the purpose of the gospel is to "present every man mature in Christ" (Col. 1:28), he gave this warning so that "no one may delude you with beguiling speech. . . . As therefore you received Christ Jesus the Lord, so live in him, rooted and built up in him, and established in the faith, just as you were taught" (Col. 2:4-7).

In other words, step 5 reminds us that there is more to the gospel than the pardon of justification, wonderful as that gift is. As we have written in earlier chapters, sanctification ("so live in him") is equally important. *Receiving* Christ and *living in Him* (verse 6) can no more be separated in the Christian life than we can separate sodium from chloride and still call it salt (NaCl).

Think carefully. How did you receive Christ Jesus as your Lord? By listening to and obeying the Holy Spirit within—the One who drew you to our Lord. How do you "live in Him"? By listening to and obeying the same Spirit within, who now creates a new world of thinking and doing. Here again, with other words, Paul describes the result of that glorious mystery, "Christ in you, the hope of glory." Earlier we saw how Paul described this process in the harvest principle, the planting of the seed of gospel truth, which we accept gladly when we "receive Christ Jesus."

But Paul keeps it simple: it's God work and our active receptivity that "grows" a Christian who has one overarching motive—to glorify God. The fulfillment of all God's promises and expectations are wrapped up in Paul's consistent promise that we be "filled with the fruits of righteousness which come through Jesus Christ" (Phil. 1:11). The *New English Bible* reads: "Reaping the full harvest of righteousness that comes through Jesus Christ." That's why "Christ in you" is the "hope of glory"—the "full harvest" that truly vindicates and thus glorifies God's patience and character in the hour of His judgment.

Now step 6: Let the wind of the Spirit blow! The Holy Spirit is the divine agent who assists us through the first five steps in making the mystery of the gospel, "Christ in you," real in our lives.

What really is happening in our neural pathways when we read the Bible, that creative Word that changes the mind of a selfish rebel into the mind "which was also in Christ Jesus" (Phil. 2:5, KJV)? Is our diligent study enough? Hardly!

Listen to this thought: "The Comforter is given that He may take of the things of Christ and show them unto us, that He may present in their rich assurance the words that fell from His lips, and convey them with living power to the soul who is obedient, who is emptied of self. It is then that the soul receives the image and superscription of the Divine. Then Christ is formed within, the hope of glory" (*Signs of the Times*, July 15, 1908).

Such is the consistent formula found throughout the Bible whenever similar phrases such as "in Christ," "through the Spirit," and "by the Spirit," are used. Experiencing the "fruits of righteousness" and "the hope of glory" are the results of a Spirit-led and empowered life (see also Romans 8). Nothing is more natural than for seed to grow when the growing conditions are right!

When we turn to God for help, He, "by the Spirit," responds by planting seeds of truth in our neural pathways. "The germ in the seed grows by the unfolding of the life-principle which God has implanted. . . . Christ implants a principle. By implanting truth and righteousness, He counterworks error and sin" (*Christ's Object Lessons*, p. 77).

"The seed has in itself a germinating principle, a principle that God Himself has implanted; yet if left to itself the seed would have no power to spring up. . . . Let man put forth his efforts to the utmost limit, he must still depend upon One who has connected the sowing and the reaping by wonderful links of His own omnipotent power" (*ibid.*, p. 63).

"In all who will submit themselves to the Holy Spirit, a new principle of life is to be implanted; the lost image of God is to be restored in humanity" (*ibid.*, p. 96).

No mystery, no involved theological discourse—just a simple picture of God planting seeds of new thoughts, new hopes, and new power in the minds of a former rebel. Does this experience happen only once in life? By no means! This planting and nurturing, this cooperation between friends, is meant to be a daily experience. This again is what Paul meant when he said, "As therefore you received Christ Jesus the Lord, so [make a life habit of living] in him" (Col. 2:6).

When we daily commit ourselves to this nurturing process, the Spirit does His mighty work—He converts the principles of truth (the seed) into thoughts and acts that reflect these implanted principles. Such thoughts and acts eventually become habitual and natural, gradually supplanting and overshadowing the bad seeds of yesteryear. Boutons in our neural pathways multiply, making the next thought and act easier, more spontaneous. This growing experience matures in a character that reveals "the full harvest of righteousness that comes through Jesus Christ"—"the hope of glory."

Many are the affirmations to this harvest principle by my favorite author: "That which at first seems difficult, by constant repetition grows easy, until right thoughts and actions become habitual" (*The Ministry of Healing*, p. 491). Or, "The principles of God's law will dwell in the heart, and control the actions. It will then be as natural for us to seek purity and holiness, to shun the spirit and example of the world, and to seek to benefit all around us, as it is for the angels of glory to execute the mission of love assigned them" (*Review and Herald*, Oct. 23, 1888).

In summary, these six steps, in making the mystery of the gospel real in our lives, work every time they are tried: 1. Recognize that our Lord is waiting for our invitation to be "in us." 2. Listen to His personal word in the Bible. 3. Let God work! 4. Respond in faith. 5. Make the glorification of God our highest motivation. 6. Let the wind of the Spirit blow!

Wherever we turn in Colossians or Philippians we see Paul emphasizing and interweaving his central theme: The open mystery of "Christ in you" (Col. 1:27) echoes his confidence we noted in our first chapter: "I am sure that he who began a good work in you will bring it to completion at the day of Jesus Christ" (Phil. 1:6).

This "good work," the purpose of the gospel, became Paul's mission statement: "that we may present every man [and woman] mature in Christ" (Col. 1:28). It could happen only when Christ is "in us."

Jesus pictured this "good work" and the process of "Christ in you" in terms of the vine and its branches (John 15). The branch is without life and worthless when detached from the vine. But when attached (as when the believer remains in the state of justification) the life power flows into the branch. Only then can the branch begin to bear fruit (as when the believer is being sanctified). Receiving Him and living in Him—becoming attached and remaining attached—is another way of describing the harvest principle, a colorful picture of how faith works.

Christians who understand God as their friend sense fully their weakness and hopelessness apart from Him. As they mature they realize even more that this connection ("Christ in you") is their only hope. That connection process is another way of describing the often misunderstood theological term *righteousness by faith.* That most important phrase could easily be described as "righteousness by connection." (This is another way of describing Paul's salvation formula that we studied in chapter 6.)

Righteousness by connection undergirds Paul's appeal in all his letters, especially in Philippians and Colossians—that they should reap "the full harvest of righteousness *that comes through* Jesus Christ." That's a real connection! "Christ in you!"

Paul's "full harvest of righteousness" corresponds to John's description of the circumstances that will exist in God's people immediately preceding the return of Jesus—in that generation when "the harvest of the earth is fully ripe" (Rev. 14:15).

John describes those people, from all over the world, who will make up this "harvest." They are those who have responded to the "call for the endurance of the saints, those who keep the commandments of God and the faith of Jesus" (verse 12). They are people who have let the formula work, who indeed invited Christ within—their only hope for glory.

This last-day harvest of righteousness becomes the final chapter in the great controversy between God and Satan. Satan never thought it could be done! This final generation, under the worst of earthly conditions, becomes part of God's convincing evidence in the days of "His" judgment—that He is not the kind of person whom Satan and others have made Him out to be.

Just to participate in these awesome events that will end history and begin eternity brings a quiet joy to the Christian. The future does not fade away into nothingness. The end, whether of our own life journey or the end climaxing in the Advent, is the beginning. The beginning of forever! The "hope of glory" realized.

Coming to Life's Fullness

11

"In Christ dwelt the fullness of the Godhead bodily. This is why, although He was tempted in all points like as we are, He stood before the world, from His first entrance into it, untainted by corruption, though surrounded by it. Are we not also to become partakers of that fullness, and is it not thus, and thus only, that we can overcome as He overcame? We lose much by not dwelling constantly upon the character of Christ" (*The SDA Bible Commentary,* Ellen G. White Comments, vol. 7, p. 907).

THE first two chapters of Colossians are fascinating because we can see how Paul's mind is working as he sets forth the essence of the gospel—God's part and our part. He has been doing this throughout Philippians and the first chapter of Colossians—but in this chapter he takes a different approach.

He first reemphasizes the centrality of Jesus Christ in the Christian's life: Jesus is the Creator of "all things . . . in heaven and on earth" (Col. 1:15). In fact, His creative power is also the continuing power that keeps all creation alive and functioning—"In him all things hold together" (verse 17). Further, in case the point is not yet clear, Paul underlined Christ's unrivaled role in the universe: "In him all the fulness of God was pleased to dwell" (verse 19). "In him the whole fulness of deity dwells bodily" (Col. 2:9).

Then he speaks to two growing problems that always need to be hit head-on. After nearly 2,000 years these two problems have never left the Christian church. They are as current today as they were in Paul's day.

The first problem is termed cheap grace, wherein professed church members want forgiveness without responsibility; the second involves professed church members who attempt to fit the gospel into their own philosophical presuppositions, making human reason the final court of appeal.

We have been responding to the first problem in previous chapters of this book. Paul comes back in Colossians 2 to hammer home his objection to cheap grace (which, from a certain viewpoint, is really a "new legalism"): "As therefore you received Christ Jesus the Lord, so live in him, rooted and built up in him and established in the faith, just as you were taught, abounding in thanksgiving" (verses 6, 7).

Paul is concerned with spiritual depth, growth, and an attitude of constantly reaching out and cooperating with God's enabling Spirit so that He can finish what He starts (Phil. 1:6) and thus "qualify" us by His "glorious might" (Col. 1:12, 11). In other words, becoming a Christian is not merely a change of mind without a difference, nor is it a mere intellectual or theoretical exercise. The personal experience of "Christ in you, the hope of glory" is light-years away from cheap grace on one hand and a philosophical adjustment on the other.

So the importance of Colossians 2:8: "See to it that no one makes a prey of you by philosophy and empty deceit, according to human tradition." Rarely has Paul been so direct against a problem in the young church, but he knew the subtle danger of looking at human reason for ultimate answers.

What is Paul's concern? He is not attacking philosophy as such in this verse. The Greek construction indicates that the "and" after "philosophy" can be better translated "even," or "the kind" that is vain. Philosophy means the "love of wisdom," and God does not want us to stop thinking about wisdom. The human mind was created with the capacity to think about the big issues, such as justice, beauty, truth, goodness, and the many "whys" of life.

In Colossae, however (and in about every church since that time), a faction attempted to answer philosophical questions without recognizing the centrality of Jesus Christ as Creator and Redeemer, as well as Lord and Saviour. Because this philosophical faction either downgraded Jesus to perhaps an angel or a remarkable man in whom "divinity" flowered, Paul correctly labeled all such philosophical speculation as "vain," or "empty deceit." If thinkers wanted to find "completeness" in their conclusions, their only route would be to recognize that Christ is "the whole fullness of deity" and that we "come to fulness of life in him" (verses 9, 10).

Of course, each new generation should rejoice in "present truth" and "advancing light"—both arenas for thoughtful men and women. But the acid test must always be the centrality of Jesus Christ, recognizing all of His functions, such as Creator, Saviour, Lord, Example, and High Priest. When anyone wants to tamper with our Lord's role as the complete answer and the all-sufficient enabler in the "great controversy" process, "wide is the gate, and broad is the way, that leadeth to destruction" (Matt. 7:13, KJV). Christianity is not "just as good" as any other religion, nor does it allow for the inclusion of practices that are alien to its purposes. Nor can we take only part of it, each deletion depending on the private opinion of "thoughtful" reasoners.

In this chapter we will look further into the second group within Colossae who were missing the "completeness" of Christ as they trusted to their several forms of legalism (Col. 2:16-3:4). But at this point let us listen in on how Paul describes what it means to recognize the bottom line of all religious thought—that "in Christ" is the center and the fullness of deity and of creative powers.

Just as Christ possessed the fullness, the completeness, of deity (not divinity, because this word has been so misused by pantheistic philosophers for thousands of years and by New Agers for decades), so Christians may have, through our Lord's "indwelling power," the fullness, the completeness, of all they need for whatever question or whatever problem in their lives. That is some thought to reflect on! Complete, nothing dangling, no problem for which we do not have a solution!

How does this happen to us individually? The answer is always the same, wherever we look in Scripture: "in Him," "with Him," "in you." Make a list of all the texts in the New Testament that use these word combinations. Paul's writings would become a riddled screen, a meaningless babble, if we took those words out of his many letters. So the following questions are on target: Are you "in Christ"? Are you walking "with Him"? Is Christ "in you, the hope of glory"?

The next question is How do we make this connection? The New Testament word by which this connection is made is "faith." Throughout his letters, Paul freely uses faith to describe the human response to the grace of God. Note Colossians 2:12: "You were buried with him in baptism, in which you were also raised with him through faith in the working of God."

Let's take a longer look at this most important word—the word that has probably been the most abused in Christian thought since the first century. To understand faith is to understand everything we have been saying so far in this book about the divine-human co-op system. Much of the confusion in understanding the phrase "righteousness by faith," whether in recent years or since the Protestant Reformation, has not been over the meaning of "righteousness." Rather, and to the surprise of many, the problem most likely resides in a person's understanding of "faith."

Misunderstanding faith separates Calvinists (Presbyterians, Reformed, etc.) from Wesleyans (Methodists, Nazarenes, etc.). In a very special way, Adventists think differently and more deeply about faith than other denominations. Because of this misunderstanding of faith, the Christian church is in conflict over such theological issues as predestination/freedom of the will; sovereignty of God/responsibility of man; atonement, either objective or subjective; nature of sin, either substantive or relational—and on and on. Each viewpoint in these theological issues has a different faith definition.

Adding to the theological confusion are the many ways we casually use the word *faith* in the English language:

1. "We don't have enough information—we must go ahead on faith." But faith is not a blind leap when all else fails.

2. "He belongs to the Baptist faith." But faith is more than a body of religious information.

3. "Keep the faith, baby!" Heard most frequently during the 1960s and early 1970s, the slogan suggests that one equates faith with deep loyalties. But Christian faith is more than intense con-

viction. Think of the devotion inspired by Adolf Hitler or Chairman Mao!

We could give other examples. Try to substitute in the phrase "righteousness by faith" the definition of faith contained in any one of those three examples. Obviously, our customary English definitions only add to theological confusion.

Part of the confusion that divides various denominations lies in our contemporary languages (English, French, German) as we try to translate the Greek words *pistis* (noun) and *pisteuein* (verb). The noun *pistis* (generally, "faith" in English) is most often translated into Latin as *fides,* into French as *foi,* and into German as *Glaube.*

But these modern languages (with the exception of German) have done something to an understanding of faith that the Greek knew better *not to* do—these languages separated the noun from the verb. Greek people reading the New Testament knew immediately that the "act of faith" (the verb action) was something that the man or woman of faith (as subject) *did!* Their language was clear: *pistis* was faith and *pisteuein* was what faith did! Something similar occurs in English—the writer writes, the swimmer swims, the fearful fear.

But not so with faith. In translating *pistis* and *pisteuein,* most modern languages separate the noun from the verb so that the connection between the two becomes unrecognizable. However, the gulf between the noun and the verb did not arise by accident. Languages do not make up words without reason. Because people eventually misunderstood the *meaning* of Christian faith, their language reflected their confusion.

For example: the Latin for *pistis* is *fides,* but its verb counterpart is *credere,* creating a serious gap of understanding, as we shall see in a moment. The French for *pistis* is *foi,* but its verb is *croire;* the English translates *pistis* with faith, and its verb counterpart (especially in the King James Version) is "to believe"!

I think you are beginning to see the problem. This unfortunate cleavage between noun and verb (which we don't have when we think of a writer who writes, a swimmer who swims, etc.) has through the centuries led the unsuspecting reader into a profound miscomprehension of the New Testament concept of faith—and thus into a faulty understanding of the plan of salvation.

For example, the Latin *credere* means to "give credit to, to assent to, a doctrine or belief." In French, *croire* means "to believe," as in believing that $2 + 2 = 4$. In English, barring a very few exceptions, in every instance in which the King James Version (and many other English translations or versions) uses "believe," it is translating *pisteuein,* the Greek verb that rightly means "to have faith."

Thus, in John 3:16, for example—"For God so loved the world that he gave his only Son, that whoever believes in him should not perish but have eternal life"—the average person would associate believe with a mental act, an intellectual acknowledgment, such as one believes that Jesus was resurrected on Sunday morning, not Tuesday morning. In other words, what does "believing in Jesus" mean? The answer is our quest in this chapter.

In German, something even more interesting—and damaging—has been done with the concept of faith. Although it has not separated the noun from the verb (*Glaube—glauben),* the linguistic tragedy still exists. Teaching the Sabbath school class to a group of Germans in North Dakota brought it forcibly to my mind—and to their attention. We were discussing faith. I asked them to tell me in German, "I have faith in Jesus." Dutifully they said, "Ich glaube an Jesus."

Then, I requested them to say, "I believe you have blue eyes." They started, "Ich glaube . . ." Pausing, they glanced at each other and tried several times, then finally one commented, "Either we have no word for believe or we have no word for faith."

Such has been the problem over the years. Even as *Glaube* has been associated only with a mental process, thus equating faith with belief and believing, so has this same misconception been part of the English and French mind as well.

When Paul and Silas told the jailer "Believe [*pisteuein*] on the Lord Jesus Christ, and thou shalt be saved" (Acts 16:31, KJV), the apostles did not mean that merely "believing" or "assenting to" the fact that Jesus was God, that He was crucified, that He promised to forgive our sins, is man's only part in the salvation process. A more accurate translation would read, "Have faith in the Lord Jesus Christ."

But if God asks for more than mental assent or conviction, *what is it?* What does faith mean?

Biblical faith is specific and unique. It embraces three acts: believe, trust, and obey God. Further, the object of faith determines its value. Thus, it is very important that what we believe, what we trust, and what we are willing to obey is really the truth!

Perhaps the only categorical biblical definition of faith appears in Hebrews 11:1: "Faith is being sure of what we hope for and certain of what we do not see" (NIV). Then to explain himself, Paul hastened to write a long chapter to picture faith in living color.

The men and women mentioned in Hebrews 11 were uncommon heroes of their generations. Although we remember them for their remarkable achievements, we must never forget that it was their faith (which they all had in common) that made them what we honor them for. For these biblical stalwarts, faith was more than mental belief, even more than enthusiasm and zeal. For the heroes of Hebrews 11, faith was the only right way to relate to God. It involved (a) a correct understanding of God's plan for them, (b) the will to respond as He wanted, and (c) an abiding trust that He would continue to do His part if human beings would do theirs.

For all the biblical heroes, faith was saying yes to God, to whatever He suggested. Faith was belief, trust, obedience, heartfelt appreciation, and deepest conviction, all wrapped up in a cheerful companionship with their Lord and Master. In other words, faith is more than merely believing—it is a happening. Something far more than thinking and feeling occurs in faith. A new power, a new attitude, takes over a Christian's life, such as reflected in the following quotation: "There is in genuine faith a buoyancy, a steadfastness of principle, and a fixedness of purpose that neither time nor toil can weaken" (*Christ's Object Lessons*, p. 147).

Perhaps the clearest statement I have ever read defining faith was written by my favorite author: "A nominal faith in Christ, which accepts Him merely as the Saviour of the world, can never bring healing to the soul. The faith that is unto salvation is not a mere intellectual assent to the truth. He who waits for entire knowledge before he will exercise faith cannot receive blessing from God. It is not enough to believe *about* Christ; we must believe *in* Him. The only faith that will benefit us is that which embraces Him as a personal Saviour; which appropriates His merits to ourselves. Many hold faith as an opinion. Saving faith is a transaction by which those who receive Christ join themselves in covenant relation with God. Genuine faith is life. A living faith means an increase of vigor, a confiding trust, by which the soul becomes a conquering power" (*The Desire of Ages*, p. 347).

If we had the space, we would say more about faith being the condition that makes salvation possible. For now, the main principle we must focus on is: faith is not the cause or initiator of salvation—grace is. But the absence of faith frustrates grace. Calvinists have misunderstood faith for centuries, thinking that faith is given only to the elect; those who truly understand the plan of salvation know that faith is not primarily God's work, but ours—the human response to God's promptings.

But after saying this, many still have a problem—even though they accept our main principle here rather than the Calvinist principle. Some of the problem lies in the way they read the text (and often the human admonition) "Have faith in God" (Mark 11:22).

They truly want to have faith in God. They try harder to have more faith so that their problems will be solved, or they believe that if they had more faith they would feel "closer" to God. But the question remains, How does one get "more" faith? How much faith does it take to "move a mountain"? How does one know when he or she has enough?

We are misreading the text if we think it says that the answer depends upon how much faith we can get into our minds or "hearts." A literal translation of the Greek would read: "Hold fast to the faithfulness of God." Ah, that's a completely different direction to look for faith. Not into your faltering heart but at the faithfulness of God, who has never failed anyone!

The clear message of Scripture, the lesson we see in the life of Jesus, is this—we are not to trust *our* faithfulness but *His* faithfulness. Others may lie to you, even disappoint you terribly—even close friends may fail you—but Jesus will not, because He is faithful. Others may back off commitments that both of you are involved in, leaving you in a tough position. Jesus will not, because He is always faithful.

Noah built an ark because he had learned that God is faithful to fulfill His promises.

Do you see more clearly what I mean concerning where we look for faithfulness? Take any of the biblical characters noted for their faith. They did what they did because they trusted God's faithfulness, not their own.

How often we estimate our difficulties in the light of our own resources, not in the light of His resources. We look at our faith, not His faithfulness. Thus, we attempt so little, and often we fail in the little we attempt.

Paul reminded the Colossians that any change of attitude, thought patterns, or conduct *since they became Christians* resulted not from their philosophical speculations, but because of their "faith in the working of God" (Col. 2:12). That's where genuine Christian faith is focused—we trust the faithfulness of God's work in and for us. That's what distinguishes that group of last-day Christians who are identified as "those who keep the commandments of God and the faith of Jesus" (Rev. 14:12).

Saying yes to whatever God has commanded and keeping our focus on the faithfulness of God—just as Jesus has shown us the way—are the divine credentials that qualify us for the wedding feast (see chapter 9 of this book) and the earmarks of the ripening harvest for which God now waits (chapter 3). Understanding faith is the key to Christian joy. Getting faith wrong can be the fly in the soup—the missing piece in the Christian's puzzle without knowing that that's the piece we should be looking for!

I guarantee it—getting faith right will clear up a lot of fog in a Christian's attempt to respond properly to their friendly Lord. I hope in this chapter that I have pierced that fog that too often seems to block out the warm rays of God's presence.

I will say it again—trust His faithfulness. He will work His plan out in you. That's His promise—and He is very good at what He does. That kind of assurance is called *joy*!

Finding Religion Without Legalism

12

"All their [the Pharisees] pretensions of piety, their human inventions and ceremonies, and even their boasted performance of the outward requirements of the law, could not avail to make them holy. They were not pure in heart or noble and Christlike in character. A legal religion is insufficient to bring the soul into harmony with God. The hard, rigid orthodoxy of the Pharisees, destitute of contrition, tenderness, or love, was only a stumbling block to sinners. They were like the salt that had lost its savor; for their influence had no power to preserve the world from corruption. The only true faith is that which 'worketh by love' (Gal. 5:6) to purify the soul. It is as leaven that transforms the character" *(Thoughts From the Mount of Blessing, p. 53).*

A S THE apostles have been telling us, the purpose of the gospel is to fulfill God's good pleasure—to "bring the soul into harmony with God" (see Phil. 2:13; Col. 1:10, 22, 23; 1 Thess. 4:1, 3, 7, 8; 1 Peter 1:14-17).

In Colossians 2:16-3:4 Paul found it necessary to warn boldly both the honestly confused and the philosopher troublemakers that "harmony with God" is found only "through faith in the working of God" (Col. 2:12), only by "holding fast to the Head, from whom the whole body, nourished and knit together through its joints and ligaments, grows with a growth that is from God" (verse 19). And nothing else!

This has been Paul's constant theme throughout all his letters: "forgiveness of sins" (Col. 1:14) and leading "a life worthy of the Lord" (verse 10) are both products of God's "glorious might" (verse 11). Christians gladly receive God's initiative, forgiveness, and sustaining power to do His will—they do not negotiate the terms.

People, at all times and in all places, have devised ways to calm their hearts so that what they were thinking or doing would somehow please God—and thus enjoy present assurance and earn eternal rewards. They wanted assurance and security on their own terms! Of course, many have done it ignorantly but sincerely, and God has His own way of dealing mercifully and appropriately with honest seekers.

But Paul is concerned with those within the Christian church who misrepresent the truth of the gospel as to how to find present assurance and to secure eternal reward.

On one hand, he was troubled by those who "insist on being saved in some way by which they may perform some important work. When they see that there is no way of weaving self into the work, they reject the salvation provided" (*The Desire of Ages*, p. 280). This group is described in Colossians 2:16-23.

On the other hand, he spoke unambiguously to those who did not practice what they preached—to those who found theological reasons whereby they would be comfortable to be saved in their sins. In our next chapter we will listen carefully to Paul as he confronts this perennial danger in the Christian church (Col. 3:5-11).

My favorite author clearly delineated these two kinds of church members who have not yet grasped the healing power of the gospel—"those who would be saved by their merits, and those who would be saved in their sins" (*The Great Controversy*, p. 572).

Before we examine Paul's counsel to those in Colossae who felt the need to add to or quantify the gospel, we should note the ages-long debate over the relationship between grace and law, especially as these words impinge on our responsibility in the salvation process. Somehow, for so many, just to mention the term *law* as an integral part of the gospel brings up all kinds of negative thoughts—especially the thought of legalism!

What does legalism mean? So many definitions afflict us. For example, many in the Christian world think that a legalist is one who believes that the laws of God are still binding on Christians; thus, any attempt to comply with God's laws becomes "righteousness by works." Or, they say, a legalist is one who hasn't learned that grace supersedes law! Let's talk about these misunderstandings.

The relationship of grace and law is just as much a front-burner issue today as it was in the church at Colossae. For instance, most Calvinists today, in contrast to Arminian/Wesleyans (where Adventists are more comfortable except for several important differences), believe that grace is God's special favor to the elect; those who are so lucky will then be given faith and the desire to submit their lives to the Lord. Sanctification and glorification are guaranteed to those who have been justified—and only the elect are justified.

However, there has always been a faction within Calvinism that goes so far as to say that sanctification is not an integral or necessary part of the salvation process; faith is essentially mental assent, a passive response to Bible truths. In fact, they make clear that sanctification is perilously close to "works-righteousness."

This ongoing conflict within Evangelicalism today (of whom most are Calvinist groups) is called the "Lordship/no-Lordship salvation" controversy. After noting that both groups are predestinarians, the debate between them is virtually identical to what the Adventist Church has been contending with for the past 30 years. Reading and listening to what John F. MacArthur, Jr., teaches as the leading representative of Lordship salvation, and to what Zane Hodges and Charles Ryrie are saying as leading spokesmen for no-Lordship salvation, one hears strange echoes of the same issues that Paul faced in every letter he wrote—and the same issues debated throughout the Adventist Church today.

Grace and law, Saviour and Lord—how shall we relate what seem to be antinomies? Is it one or the other—as so many would choose? Or are both important, as some say, but one is more important than the other?

As with the two foci of an ellipse: to remove one focus makes the ellipse into a circle—the ellipse is no more. But with the plan of salvation, each focus has equal weight, equal function. When anyone places more weight, more value, on one focus and in some way diminishes the other, we make a circle out of the ellipse. We are left with only a half-truth—which is a total error.

Paul frequently connects grace with law as two sides of the same coin. At other times he contrasts the two, especially when he is referring to Jewish ritual law (see Rom. 4:16; 5:20; 6:14, 15; Gal. 2:21; 5:4). But never does Paul state that grace nullifies the Ten Commandments—much to the contrary (Rom. 6:14, 15; 3:31). Grace is God's enabling power to accomplish what the law demands (Rom. 5:21; 8:1-39)!

The Adventist position has always been that Christians will joyfully comply with the Ten Commandments (and anything else God has commanded) as their part in the divine-human co-op, without which salvation would not happen. Unfortunately for some the dilemma has been obedience—how much obedience or how little, if any? What kind of human responsibility is involved in "walking as Christ walked"? A misunderstanding here can be fatal unless corrected. Such were the issues in 1888 at the Minneapolis General Conference session.

When considering the relationship between Christ's role as Saviour and Lord, I have never seen it better put than in the following words—words written to help clarify the 1888 issues: "Let this point be fully settled in every mind: If we accept Christ as a Redeemer, we must accept Him as a Ruler. We cannot have the assurance and perfect confiding trust in Christ as our Saviour until we acknowledge Him as our King and are obedient to His commandments. Thus we evidence our allegiance to God. We have then the genuine ring in our faith, for it is a working faith. It works by love" (*Faith and Works*, p. 16).

Understanding the issues of 1888 will greatly simplify and strengthen our personal response to God's call for a special people with a special message for a special time. One of our church's thought leaders said in his latest book that the central challenge facing our church today is its "identity crisis" (see Jack Provonsha, *A Remnant in Crisis* [Hagerstown, Md.: Review and Herald Pub. Assn., 1993], pp. 7, 166).

More precisely, he says, the present crisis is primarily a matter of what the "message" is—because "a prophetic movement derives its mission and reason for being from its message. To be true to God's call, then, this movement should be clear about what it has to say. . . . It especially concerns those truths that represent truth's progression at its growing edge" (*ibid.*, p. 167).

Adventism's present challenge is to recapture the "vitalizing energy of our movement's early years," and that "depends upon our being able to see again—in our time—the essence of what seemed so clear in theirs" (*ibid.*, p. 62).

In 1888 the essence of Adventism's recovery of lost or compromised biblical truths was clearly stated. (We note this 1888 episode because it bears directly on the issue of legalism.) Many are the references of the 1880s depicting a bleak picture of a languishing spiritual condition throughout the Adventist Church. This "Laodicean" condition was partly because of our early preachers focusing on the Sabbath and the soon return of Jesus, while assuming that justification by faith was an unspoken assumption that everyone believed. In addition, because of the focus on the seventh-day Sabbath, nineteenth-century Adventists read the words but forgot the music—they slipped into thinking that "keeping the commandments" automatically was the same as "loving God." This silent shift eroded Christian experience and beclouded an intimate personal relationship with Jesus.

In speaking to ministers at that time, Ellen White said: "Too often this truth is presented in cold theory. . . . A theory of the truth without vital godliness cannot remove the moral darkness which envelops the soul" (*Testimonies*, vol. 4, pp. 313, 314). What had happened is that our church, generally, had drifted into a legalistic experience, holding fast to their commandmentkeeping. But a rich, Spirit-filled life—a heart religion—that moves people from one victory over sin to another was sadly lacking.

Consequently, the world had not been given a fair picture of what the messages of the three angels was meant to be. Therefore, the need for a reemphasis in 1888: "The message [brought by Jones and Waggoner] of the gospel of His grace was to be given to the church in clear and distinct lines, that the world should no longer say that Seventh-day Adventists talk the law, the law, but do not teach or believe Christ" (*Testimonies to Ministers*, p. 92).

What follows may be the most informing description of the 1888 focus on the uniqueness of the Adventist message (it really had not been so explicitly set forth since the days of Paul): "The Lord in His great mercy sent a most precious message to His people through Elders Waggoner and Jones. This message was to bring more prominently before the world the uplifted Saviour, the sacrifice for the sins of the whole world. It presented justification through faith in the Surety; it invited the people to receive the righteousness of Christ, which is made manifest in obedience to all the commandments of God. Many had lost sight of Jesus. They needed to have their eyes directed to His divine person, His merits, and His changeless love for the human family. All power is given into His hands, that He may dispense rich gifts unto men, imparting the priceless gift of His own righteousness to the helpless human agent. This is the message that God commanded to be given to the world. It is the third angel's message, which is to be proclaimed with a loud voice, and attended with the outpouring of His Spirit in a large measure" (*ibid.*, pp. 91, 92).

Surely "a most precious message" that, if proclaimed fully, would become "a loud voice [cry]" to finish God's work on earth—surely the fullness of that message of hope—should be the subject of highest priority for every Adventist today.

The point I am making here is that the coldness of nineteenth-century orthodoxy that prevailed generally in Protestantism eventually overcame zealous Adventists. The result: "too many Christless sermons preached" (*Review and Herald*, Oct. 8, 1889). Legalism prevailed!

When legalism prevails, discouragement and spiritual depression soon follow. Intent on being Christians, legalists (most often unknowingly) see only rigor, demand, and checklists. Jesus as their personal Saviour, their personal enabler, their closest friend, as faithful high priest, becomes obscured. Though such church members desire to please God, they feel only the pressure and see only the cloud.

Those who do keep up their courage believe they must try harder, thinking that that's the way to find peace. (Here again is a good example of not understanding the full meaning of "faith" and "trusting in God's faithfulness.") Inadvertently, they become more focused on lawkeeping than on the Christ of the law. They become even more circumspect in their business dealings, in their Sabbathkeeping, in their dress, in their TV watching, and whatever else.

All this is most commendable in a day of unbridled license, in which moral standards seem to have evaporated. But there is no joy in this kind of religion—no matter how much approval they may be rightly receiving from those who are blessed with such good behavior. However, more rigor—more devotion to even Bible study and prayer—is not the answer to the joyless heart of a legalist!

The answer to cold legalism was clearly presented in the "precious message" that Elders Jones and Waggoner and Ellen White brought to the 1888 General Conference session and in various books and sermons after that momentous date. That message was not a "get-ready-or-else" threat, but tremendous good news as to "how" to get ready. It restored Jesus as one who was very "near" to His people, near even before sinners realized the Godhead's love for them. He was seen as one who, in His human nature, completely identified with fallen men and women (see chapter 5), who showed us how we may become conquerors over sin. His role as our high priest was given a clear focus in the 1888 messages as a vital element in helping us to overcome our sins as we help to close the great controversy.

Perhaps, the golden thread of this "good news" (to which Ellen White, in response, said, "Every fiber of my heart said, Amen" [*The Ellen G. White 1888 Materials*, vol. 1, p. 349]) is this thought: Our standing with God does not depend upon our rigor or even our initiative in claiming His promises, but on our willingness to receive what He has already provided—and that He will continue to provide salvation for us, if we do not frustrate His will. That thought stands legalism on its head!

A haunting warning hangs over all of us today as we relate in some manner to this "precious message" that remains perennially relevant: "I have no smooth message to bear to those who have been so long as false guideposts, pointing the wrong way. If you reject Christ's delegated messengers, you reject Christ. Neglect this great salvation, kept before you for years, despise this glorious offer of justification through the blood of Christ and sanctification through the cleansing power of the Holy Spirit, and there remaineth no more sacrifice for sins, but a certain fearful looking for of judgment and fiery indignation" (*Testimonies to Ministers*, pp. 97, 98).

Some say, with plenty of justification, that our problem in the Adventist Church today is not legalism but rampant license. Perhaps, and we will speak to that in our next chapter. But the sly, subtle, ever-present inclination toward legalism resides as a virus in every religious body—corporately and individually— ready to multiply into open disease unless the immune system is kept healthy. Especially within any person who knows that "pleasing God" involves "commandmentkeeping."

During my 45 years of ministry in many areas, I have been able to spot early symptoms of the emerging virus, or its full-growth manifestation, which I can sum up in two words—no joy! Lots of church activity, lots of personal sacrifice—but no joy! This is sad—and probably the reason why I am making an extended point in this chapter regarding the subtle danger of legalism. Adventists, with all their responsibilities, need joy, if anyone does! And joy is free! It is the easiest glow to enjoy!

Listen slowly, carefully, to the following words: "Some who come to God by repentance and confession, and even believe that their sins are forgiven, still fail of claiming, as they should, the promises of God. They do not see that Jesus is an ever-present Saviour; and they are not ready to commit the keeping of their souls to Him, relying upon Him to perfect the work of grace begun in their hearts [think of our chapter 3]. While they think they are committing themselves to God, there is a great deal of self-dependence. There are conscientious souls that trust partly to God and partly to themselves [this does not contradict Paul's words in Philippians 2:12, etc., as we studied in chapter 6]. They do not look to God, to be kept by His power, but depend upon watchfulness against temptation and the performance of certain duties for acceptance with Him. There are no victories in this kind of faith. Such persons toil to no purpose; their souls are in continual bondage; and they find no rest until their burdens are laid at the feet of Jesus.

"There is need of constant watchfulness and of earnest, loving devotion, but these will come naturally when the soul is kept by the power of God through faith. . . . Love springs up in the heart. There may be no ecstasy of feeling, but there is an abiding, peaceful trust. Every burden is light; for the yoke which Christ imposes is easy. Duty becomes a delight, and sacrifice a pleasure. . . . This is walking in the light as Christ is in the light" (*Faith and Works,* pp. 38, 39).

Those two paragraphs describe joy! Take time for a second reading!

All this and probably more needed to be said before we listen to Paul speak to those Colossians who were entrapped in legalisms, either because of philosophical speculation or a confused understanding of how Christians should be commandmentkeepers without being legalists.

You will notice many references to ritualism of some kind, even the God-given ritualism of the Old Testament. Ritualism, properly understood, has its place—such as saluting our country's flag or treading softly in the church sanctuary. But we don't earn God's favor through ritualism; we acknowledge receiving it. Even Sabbathkeeping, especially its edges, can become a ritualistic rigor that profits nothing—if we are not remembering that the Sabbath is a delight, that its Maker is our best friend, and that we do what we do to bring honor to Him.

You will pause in Colossians 2:23. Adventists especially must think carefully about their attention to health principles and ask, Why am I a vegetarian? Why do I avoid tobacco and alcoholic beverages, even caffeine products? Is it primarily a sense of demand— "I must be a faithful health reformer to gain God's approval"?

The answer, of course, is yes and no. No in the sense that God already has reconciled Himself to you (2 Cor. 5:18, 19)—what you do does not change His love for you. No in the sense that the purpose of health reform is not primarily to please God, but to take His advice as to how to live a happy, healthy, holy life. Yes in the sense that all parents enjoy seeing their children take their counsel. Parents give counsel because they love their children and want to see them avoid terrible mistakes. When children take advice readily, obviously their parents are happy and approve what they are doing. Yes, God does love us unconditionally. No, God does not approve what we do unconditionally. God is not happy to see us destroy ourselves, or even to diminish our potential.

The one question that may help all of us think carefully about the cloud of legalism is this: Am I keeping the Sabbath, paying tithe, and giving Bible studies to impress God or to honor Him? The answer may take some thought. The question needs to be asked every day as time goes on.

The sad part of legalism is that so much religious activity is external, superficial, and done to impress—thus, not heart religion. Legalism has "an appearance of wisdom in promoting rigor of devotion and self-abasement" (Col. 2:23). The outside impresses others—perhaps evoking admiration. But the heart has not changed—its "indulgences" are unchecked (verse 23).

Our Lord's dealings with the Pharisees (Matt. 6) helps us here: "The spirit of Pharisaism is the spirit of human nature. . . . In the days of Christ the Pharisees were continually trying to earn the favor of Heaven in order to secure the worldly honor and prosperity which they regarded as the reward of virtue. At the same time they paraded their acts of charity before the people in order to attract their attention and gain a reputation for sanctity" (*Thoughts From the Mount of Blessing*, p. 79).

Legalism may or may not spring from the right motive. Apparently, many of the Pharisees operated from a self-centered motive. Many struggling Christians have the right motive but live in legalism gloom. Sad! They need to hear the good news! They don't need to relax their commandmentkeeping; they need to take the hand of Him who provides the inner strength and the continuing willingness to be joyfully obedient to their heavenly Friend. They need to see God as their friend, not as a severe taskmaster. They need to sense the joy of letting Christ live "in" them, the only "hope of glory" (Col. 1:27). They need to hang their helpless souls on their great Friend, who never lets go!

This is what Paul meant when he next urged the Colossians to "set your minds on things that are above. . . . Your life is hid with Christ in God" (Col. 3:2).

Over the years "faithful" legalists have given their best to the church—but not much joy! In fact, for more than a century a good percentage of Adventist tithes and offerings have come from the pockets of legalists! In contrast with church members who want the "blessing" without the responsibility of genuine faith-obedience, who can belittle all this giving, this unselfishness?

Yet with all this devotion we may have heard the words without the music. Without a clear understanding of God as friend, without a genuine companionship with our Enabling Spirit, the journey is hard, duty without the pleasure. Hard-working, responsible fathers and mothers and loyal church members deserve to hear the good news of Colossians.

Somehow I hope that this chapter has helped. No one knows joy more than those who have united commandmentkeeping with the faith of Jesus. What God hath joined together, let no one put asunder!

Finding Religion Without License

13

"It is not enough for us to believe that Jesus is not an imposter, and that the religion of the Bible is no cunningly devised fable. We may believe that the name of Jesus is the only name under heaven whereby man may be saved, and yet we may not through faith make Him our personal Saviour. It is not enough to believe the theory of truth. It is not enough to make a profession of faith in Christ and have our names registered on the church roll. 'He that keepeth his commandments dwelleth in him, and he in him. And hereby we know that he abideth is us, by the Spirit which he hath given us.' 'Hereby we do know that we know him, if we keep his commandments' (1 John 3:24; 2:3). This is the genuine evidence of conversion. Whatever our profession, it amounts to nothing unless Christ is revealed in works of righteousness" *(Christ's Object Lessons,* pp. 312, 313).

IN CHAPTER 12 we noted that Paul made clear that we must not nullify grace and corrupt the Christian life by legalism. In this chapter, as we focus on Colossians 3:5-11, Paul's concern is that we must not nullify grace and corrupt the Christian life by licentiousness.

After reading these six verses, we are forced to ask the question To whom might Paul be talking? He uses very strong words, and his warnings are heavy indeed.

Obviously, this letter to the Colossians is a letter to young Christians, not to the unchurched. Those who read this letter together at worship on some Sabbath morning (or possibly listened to it being read in some isolated mountain home) were professed church members. They were baptized church members, a fact that Paul emphasized in Colossians 2.

Apparently some members at Colossae were confused regarding the gospel (as so many are today). Somehow they were led to believe that Christianity was a change without a difference. How could it be that Christians who knew the teachings of Jesus would think that their behavior did not affect their relationship with God—or that behavior had no relationship to the preaching of the gospel? This theological twist (so different from Christ's words regarding the behavior expected from those who chose to follow Him) has been termed, by some, the "new legalism." From one standpoint, the term is an accurate one.

We see the fallout from the new legalism wherever we look today. Symptoms of this theological virus are noted when people are preoccupied with a legal adjustment of one's standing with God without an equal concern for the life behavior that should correspond with their new allegiance—and with their acceptance of God's offer of forgiveness.

The new legalism hangs perilously on the cliffs of antinomianism (that is, God's law is not binding on the "saved"; behavior is unrelated to faith, etc.). Antinomianism inevitably arises when human responsibility in the divine-human co-op plan is discounted, or where the results of grace are restricted to the acts of God alone.

I must make it clear that not all antinomians speak with equal emphasis when they tend to minimize Christian behavior as an integral part of the salvation process. John F. MacArthur, Jr., one of the leading spokesmen for Lordship salvation among Evangelicals today, writes: "To say someone is antinomian is not necessarily to say that person spurns holiness or condones ungodliness. Most antinomians vigorously appeal for Christians to walk in a manner worthy of their calling; but at the same time they minimize the relationship between obedience and faith. Antinomians typically believe Christians *should yield* to the Lordship of Christ; they just do not believe surrender is a binding requirement in the gospel call to faith. Antinomians do not necesssarily despise the law of God; they simply believe it is irrelevant to saving faith. They suggest that obedience to the righteous principles of the law might not become a pattern in the Christian's life (cf. Rom. 8:4; 10:4). In short, antinomianism is the belief that allows for justification without sanctification. Antinomianism makes obedience elective" (*Faith Works* [Dallas: Word Publishing, 1993], p. 95).

Perhaps we see evidence of the new legalism when we hear half-truths such as "You can't keep the law this side of the resurrection—we have sinful flesh until then"; "You don't have to keep the law because Jesus kept it for you"; "You shouldn't try to keep the law—it just leads to discouragement and legalism." All these comments result from either using biblical texts out of context or completely misunderstanding the biblical definitions of such vital concepts as faith and grace. Assuredly, such comments do not consider passages such as Colossians 3:5-11. (See also Rom. 8:13; Gal. 5:24; Eph. 4:19; 5:3-5.)

In short, the new legalism is more concerned with a change in one's legal standing with God than with a change in one's behavior that befits those who "walk not according to the flesh but according to the Spirit" (Rom. 8:4). Faith, to the new legalist, is a matter of believing (as we studied in chapter 12) without the content of obedience. (Somehow the intent of Hebrews 5:8, 9 is overlooked: "Although he was a Son, he learned obedience through what he suffered; and being made perfect he became the source of eternal salvation to all who obey him.")

We note the ramifications of new legalism when we hear such thoughts as "The future can hold no possible condemnation for the man who has received the work of Christ on the cross" or "Be assured, your future judgment was already decided in your favor on the cross." This kind of thinking is exactly what John Wesley said had to be cut out at the root, adding often his contention that we do not make a leap from justification to heaven by bypassing sanctification.

Let's follow Paul's counsel more closely: Because you have "set your minds on things that are above" (Col. 3:2), because "Christ . . . is our life" (verse 4), "put to death therefore what is earthly in you" (verse 5).

Warning: Here Paul is not giving substance to the Grecian

error that has infiltrated most of Christianity—that the soul (the spiritual element in us) is separate from the body, that there is no psychosomatic relationship, one affecting the other. For the Greek philosopher, to discipline the body, to deprive it of pleasure or even comfort, is to nurture the soul. Thus, persons who embrace the "immortal soul" principle are candidates for the new legalism; with a different twist of thinking, such persons also set themselves up for the old legalism of Colossians 2:16-23.

In Colossians 3 Paul is simply recognizing that Christianity is a matter of moral responsibility on the human side, not a matter of spiritual bookkeeping whereby heavenly entries are made that do not reflect truthfully what is happening on earth. They misunderstand the nature of justification or faith, as we have discussed in earlier chapters. To make our point quickly as we move on, let us note these pointed clarifications by my favorite author: "No one can believe with the heart unto righteousness, and obtain justification by faith, while continuing the practice of those things which the Word of God forbids, or while neglecting any known duty. . . . It is by continual surrender of the will, by continual obedience, that the blessing of justification is retained. . . . It is an evidence that a man is not justified by faith when his works do not correspond to his profession" (*Selected Messages*, book 1, pp. 396, 397).

Some Colossians had not yet "put to death" those earthly practices common to unconverted persons. The Greek makes clear that Paul was very emphatic: "Put to death, once and for all . . ."

Do we have to wonder what Paul meant by "earthly"? (Compare Paul's longer list in Galatians 5:19-21.) The following words are in apposition to "earthly"—that is, they expand on what Paul means:

"Immorality"—a general Greek word that includes all illicit sexual behavior.

"Impurity"—anything that would morally defile.

"Passion"—in the New Testament this word is always used in a negative sense, thus depraved lust.

"Evil desire"—the Greek word for "desire" can be used for good aspirations as well as evil, and that's why Paul used the adjective "evil."

"Covetousness"—the Greek word is most picturesque, describing the ever-reaching craving for more. Paul's designation of covetousness as idolatry recognizes the severe sickness of "never having enough." How many homes, churches, communities, and nations have been ruined because someone or a group wanted more power or money than they had earned. They would take that which did not belong to them. Surely, whatever becomes so important that it becomes the number one goal of a person's life is properly labeled "idolatry."

Then Paul introduces a word, "wrath," that has been sorely fought over throughout Christian history, even to this very moment. What philosophical presuppositions do people have that compels them to take such opposite positions as to what God's wrath must be?

I like the straightforward biblical picture best—it conforms to the entire story from Genesis to Revelation. *The SDA Bible Commentary* (vol. 6, pp. 477, 478) nicely summarizes the biblical phrase "wrath of God":

The wrath of God is "the divine displeasure against sin, resulting ultimately in the abandonment of man to the judgment of death. . . . God's wrath against sin is exercised in the withdrawal of His presence and life-giving power from those who choose to remain in sin and thus share in its inevitable consequences. . . .

"When God's wrath against sin fell upon Christ as our substitute, it was the separation from His Father that caused Him such great anguish. 'This agony He must not exert His divine power to escape. As man He must suffer the consequence of man's sin. As man He must endure the wrath of God against transgression' (*The Desire of Ages*, p. 686). . . .

"Thus, as Paul explains in Romans 1:24, 26, 28, God reveals His wrath by turning impenitent men over to the inevitable results of their rebellion. This persistent resistance of God's love and mercy culminates in the final revelation of God's wrath on that day when the Spirit of God is at last withdrawn. . . .

"But even this final revelation of God's wrath in the destruction of the wicked is not an act of arbitrary power. 'God is the fountain of life; and when one chooses the service of sin, he separates from God, and thus cuts himself off from life' (*The Desire of Ages*, p. 764). God gives men existence for a time so that they may develop their characters. When this has been accomplished, they receive the results of their own choice. 'By a life of rebellion, Satan and all who unite with him place themselves so out of harmony with God that His very presence is to them a consuming fire' (*ibid.; cf. The Great Controversy*, p. 543)."

Obviously, Paul is not treating the sins of the unconverted lightly, especially when they are still being practiced by professed church members!

But Paul is not through. He now turns to the "sins of the saints," from the gross sins of immorality to the equally destructive sinful practices that may not be as sensational or visible as the previous set of four. He uses strong language, as seen better in the Greek: "Strip yourselves, once and for all, of these filthy garments!"

Now follows five attitudes, all expressed through the mouth, sort of a list of rampant social diseases: anger (a fast-triggered response to whatever does not please), wrath (a boiling agitation, probably explosive), malice (ill will, with perhaps a desire to hurt), slander (speech that injures another's good name), and foul talk (low, obscene speech). No wonder James had so much to say about bridling the mouth (James 3:3-12)!

Then Paul adds another characteristic of confused church members who believe they are covered by God's righteousness while still making a habit of lying when they please. I find it interesting that he makes a special effort, with strong language, to focus on this human weakness: "Please, stop your lying!"

Lying is so prevalent wherever one turns. In that remarkable book *The Day America Told the Truth*, research indicated: "Just about everyone lies—91 percent of us lie regularly. The majority of us find it hard to get through a week without lying. One in five can't make it through a single day—and we're talking about conscious, premeditated lies.

"When we refrain from lying, it's less often because we think it's wrong (only 45 percent) than for a variety of other reasons, among them the fear of being caught (17 percent).

"We lie to just about everyone, and the better we know someone, the likelier we are to have told them a serious lie.

"Who lies the most in America? Men lie more than women; young men lie more than older men; gays and bisexuals lie more than heterosexuals; Blacks lie more than Whites, Catholics lie a bit more than Protestants, and both lie more than Jews; unemployed people lie more than those with jobs; the poor lie more than the rich; and liberals lie more than conservatives" (pp. 45-47).

Now Paul turns toward the positive side of the converted life. On the way he did his best to remove the possible charge of personal opinion in his imperatives for changed behavior. The one standard Paul put before the early Christian church as a benchmark of acceptable behavior was "the image of [the] creator" (Col. 3:10). Paul was not deflected by debates over perfectionism or works-righteousness—throughout his writings he hammers away at the example of Jesus, our Creator, as the model person.

He continues his garment metaphor: "Put on the garment of the new man which is being renewed by a continually expanded, experiential knowledge which is according to the image of the One who created him" (literal translation).

In other words, Paul is saying, "Would Jesus lie? Would He use foul language? Would He harbor anger, wrath, malice, and slander? Would you ever expect Jesus to be a homosexual or a fornicator or covetous?" Putting it that way, Paul surely had the attention of his Colossian readers.

Paul is saying, "Don't talk to me about your family traits that 'make you what you are.' Don't tell me that because you come from a particular country, 'your conduct or disposition is the way it is where you come from.'"

Why could Paul be so unrelenting about the Christian's challenge to overcome all inherited or acquired tendencies to sin? Because whether you are a Greek or Jew, circumcised or uncircumcised, barbarian, Scythian, slave, free man—or whoever else—if you really understand the gospel, "Christ is all and in all." If He is "in you" (there's that phrase again), you will learn what it means to live as He did, no matter who you are or where you came from! The new legalists have difficulty with Colossians 3!

Paul's words are powerful! That rifle-shot logic is formidable! The point is unescapable! If perhaps anyone is still thinking that they may want a second chance someday "to get it right," listen again to Paul. These verses contain definite imperatives to be acted upon immediately. We are getting our second chances every day of our lives. For some of us it may be the 1,539,098th chance! Let's get this one right by using Paul's formula, "Christ in you, the hope of glory" (Col. 1:27).

As for those who are truly seeking joy in their lives, they will take Paul's advice. They have asked their waiting Father to help them remove the old garments of sinful conduct and replace them with the garments of Christ's righteousness. They know from experience that this "putting off" and "putting on" is not a paper transaction in heaven alone. They now know what it means to be ready for the wedding (see chapter 9). They now have joy, letting the Bridegroom help them to get ready for the wedding!

Making Christianity Real

14

"The gospel is to be presented, not as a lifeless theory, but as a living force to change the life. God desires that the receivers of His grace shall be witnesses to its power. Those whose course has been most offensive to Him He freely accepts; when they repent, He imparts to them His divine Spirit, places them in the highest positions of trust, and sends them forth into the camp of the disloyal to proclaim His boundless mercy. He would have His servants bear testimony to the fact that through His grace men may possess Christlikeness of character, and may rejoice in the assurance of His great love. He would have us bear testimony to the fact that He cannot be satisfied until the human race are reclaimed and reinstated in their holy privileges as His sons and daughters" *(The Desire of Ages,* p. 826).

IN COLOSSIANS 3:12-4:1 Paul turns from his concern for eliminating unbefitting conduct to the bright, positive side of how Christians ought to be perceived by everyone watching their growth.

Through the years I have heard, "No one should tell me how to live. If my heart is right, it's no one else's business what I do!" Usually, these words are said under deep conviction while one is wrestling with a long-standing dispositional problem. Just as often, people say it is a characteristic that "runs in the family." And I agree, it's not easy to uproot.

Usually my response has been: "You are right! That's not my business, except when asked. But do me a favor—read four short letters in the New Testament—Galatians, Ephesians, Philippians, and Colossians, and talk to God about it. Then tell me what you think." More times than not, the issue is resolved.

Paul is not bashful about how his fellow church members ought to live. He tells them what they must *not* be known for (Col. 3:5-11), and now he outlines forthrightly what they *should* be known for.

He rises above his personal opinion. Using three well-known Old Testament terms, he appeals to the young Christian church to grasp their mission as the new Israel—God's chosen ones. What a responsibility! As chosen ones they are set apart for a holy purpose; they are God's beloved. What an introduction as the apostle challenges church members to make Christianity real in a secularized, degraded world! For the Christian, what could be higher motivation then and now?

Again we have Paul's metaphor of clothing, "Put on, once and for all . . ." This act is not something that God can do without the Christian's cooperation. God can prompt and plead, but He cannot put our clothes on for us! God can supply the air, but we must do our own breathing! God is very powerful, but He cannot put your Christian clothes on for you—that's where He needs your cooperation.

The next few verses sound like the Christian's résumé. We live in a day when résumés are most important. Men and women, by the tens of thousands, have worked for decades, perhaps at the top of their careers—only to discover that they are part of the downsizing of their company. Although they have no job, they still have the usual mortgage and car payments to make, and perhaps aged parents as well as their children to care for. They need a job! One of their best options is to mail out their résumés!

High school graduates and college seniors are also flooding the mail these days with their résumés—as they describe who they are and how they can make some employer happy!

Would your personal résumé look like the Christian résumé that Paul has created for you in these Colossian passages?

All these precious characteristics of a genuine Christian are expressions of the many facets of love as seen under varying circumstances. In other words, a Christian should not be known for meekness if at the same time he or she is not kind. Or a truly converted Christian would be a contradiction if he or she were patient but also known for an unforgiving spirit. That is why Paul colorfully pictures "love" (verse 14) as "ligaments" that "bind everything together in perfect harmony." (Just think how your arms and legs would function without the ligaments holding everything together.) This passage is similar to Paul's words in Romans 13:10: "Love is the fulfilling of the law."

In other words, Paul needed to add this binding quality of love to his list of beautiful virtues because it is altogether possible to "appear" compassionate, humble, etc., and still be without genuine love, as Jesus would love. Think of the hypocrite examples in our Lord's sermon on the mount!

Most of the virtues (Col. 3:12, 13) are words or attitudes that are clearly understood. But probably not the English words "bowels of mercies" (KJV) or "compassion" (RSV).

In Matthew 14 we read about a busy day in the life of Jesus. Trying to get away from the crowds for some rest, He discovered that the multitudes anticipated His "quiet place." Though weary (for many good reasons), "he had compassion on them" (verse 14).

The Greek word translated here as "compassion" or "bowels of mercy" in Colossians 3:12 is a much deeper word than the Greek words for "pity" or "sympathy." Compassion *is* more than pity or sympathy. The Greek root word translated compassion is known in the medical world as viscera; "splanchnology" is the study of the visceral parts, or the gut. The blood flow through the viscera and then through the liver is called the "splanchnic circulation."

What does this have to do with compassion? When Jesus saw the fathers and mothers with their children pressing Him with their troubles, He felt their hurt in His gut. He was moved in the stomach by their needs. He felt their needs and forgot His own. Have you ever felt that deeply about someone else's problem—even to having your stomach and bowels upset? That's compassion!

"Forbearing"—what does that word mean? The Greek helps: "holding yourselves back from one another." Sounds like good advice for members at some committee meetings I have attended! Solomon said it well: "A soft answer turns away wrath" (Prov. 15:1). Paul and Solomon are correct—their counsel works!

The next unambiguous appeal is to make a practice out of "forgiving each other; as the Lord has forgiven you" (Col. 3:13). "As"—that is a very small word with a tremendous implication. Think of these other similar phrases throughout the New Testament:

"Whoever would be first among you must be your slave; even as the Son of man came not to be served but to serve" (Matt. 20:27, 28).

"A new commandment I give to you, that you love one another; even as I have loved you" (John 13:34).

"Keep them in thy name . . . that they may be one, even as we are one. . . . They are not of the world, even as I am not of the world" (John 17:11-14).

"Walk in love, as Christ loved us" (Eph. 5:2).

"He who says he abides in him ought to walk in the same way in which he walked." "Every one who thus hopes in him purifies himself as he is pure." "We may have confidence for the day of judgment, because as he is so are we in this world" (1 John 2:6; 3:3; 4:17).

When anyone suggests to us that our behavior has nothing to do with our salvation, think carefully and quietly about these texts that clearly set forth the Christian agenda: to serve, to love, to relate to the world, to be one in unity, to walk, to purify oneself—*as Jesus did!* Keep your theology simple—just keep your eye on Jesus and your ears open to what He said!

Paul goes even deeper in writing the Christian's résumé: "Let the peace of Christ rule in your hearts, to which indeed you were called in the one body" (Col. 3:15). What insight! Paul had already appealed for kindness, for forbearance, for a forgiving spirit—he knew that factions and strife existed in Colossae and in every other young church. He knew that without seeking these virtues as personal habits, no church member would have peace—no tranquillity of soul.

But with this emphasis on peace in relation to the "body," Paul recognizes the higher principle. Without first finding inward peace, without letting the spirit of Jesus be the "umpire" of conflict within the Christian's troubled mind, the external strife between church members would never cool down. That's why appeals for church unity seem so futile if the individual items on the agenda are not first resolved.

Pause for a moment and think: only the gentle, sweet spirit of the peace of Jesus can calm our troubled hearts. Only the wisdom of His Spirit, as the Fair Umpire, can open our eyes so that we can see the bigger picture wherein our kindness, our compassion, our humility, our forbearance, and our forgiveness are the elements to bring closure to our inner turmoil and to church agitation. Let the Spirit of Christ be the arbitrator and answer to all strife, all hurt feelings, all seemingly irreconcilable human relationships!

Almost as if it is so obvious that he almost forgot, Paul adds: "And be thankful" (verse 15). Herein lies not only the secret of joy under tough times but also the greatest health principle in the universe: "Gratitude, rejoicing, benevolence, trust in God's love and care—these are health's greatest safeguards" (*The Ministry of Healing*, p. 281).

The only way by which all these Christian characteristics can be developed in "growing" church members is to "let the word of Christ dwell in you richly." Reread our discussion in chapter 10 of how reading the Word is akin to letting the Word of God do something creative in our lives. Yes, I am joining together what I think Paul joins—the written Word becomes the vehicle for the Living Word to do His promised work within us. The development of this wonderful thought requires another book!

One of Paul's towering summations now follows his exhortations: "Whatever you do, . . . do everything in the name of the Lord Jesus" (verse 17). The highest response to what our friendly Lord is waiting to do for, in, and through us is to return the favor—in our sphere. Paul made it clear throughout his writings, reflecting the many warnings of Jesus that becoming His disciple is a tough march in a hostile world. But we brace ourselves against the wind, we lengthen our stride, and with a song in our heart (verse 16) we "do" (that's the word, "do") everything that would bear faithful witness to the "name of the Lord Jesus." (See our Lord's warning in Matthew 7:21-28.) What an assignment! What a privilege!

Listen to my favorite author again: "When the Spirit of God controls mind and heart, the converted soul breaks forth into a new song; for he realizes that in his experience the promise of God has been fulfilled, that his transgression has been forgiven, his sin covered. He has exercised repentance toward God for the violation of the divine law, and faith toward Christ. . . .

"But because this experience is his, the Christian is not therefore to fold his hands, content with that which has been accomplished for him. He who has determined to enter the spiritual kingdom will find that all the powers and passions of unregenerate nature, backed by the forces of the kingdom of darkness, are arrayed against him. Each day he must renew his consecration, each day do battle with evil. Old habits, hereditary tendencies to wrong, will strive for the mastery, and against these he is to be ever on guard, striving in Christ's strength for victory" (*The Acts of the Apostles*, pp. 476, 477).

After all Paul's counsel regarding what it means for the Christian to "do, in word and deed, . . . everything in the name of the Lord" (Col. 3:17), he puts the floodlight on those areas where the apostle knows his counsel is most needed—the Christian home and the Christian workplace (verses 18-25). If harmony and mutual objectives are languishing in these primary areas of life, the church will be in turmoil because of pent-up frustrations in its members, or it will suffocate because of hurting, depressed members. Many are the books that are especially helpful in both these primary areas of everyone's life—a literary genre that didn't even exist 30 or 40 years ago! Read them and be blessed!

"Whatever you do . . ." On August 4, 1892, a young British surgeon landed on the bleak coast of Labrador. This dismal, subarctic place became his home until he died at 75. We know him today as Sir Wilfred Grenfell. But we never would have known him if he had not turned his back on a promising professional career in the fashionable Mayfair section of London. After his very successful schooling at Oxford, his friends thought he had lost his mind when he ventured to go to Labrador. He had too much to offer London—why waste his personality, skills, and a guaranteed future on a few unlettered and unknown fishermen along the icebound, uncharted coast of a faraway place?

But in 1892, at the young age of 27, this man said to Labrador, "What I do, in word or deed, I do everything in the name of the Lord Jesus."

What sparked a man like Wilfred Grenfell? Was he an eccentric who enjoyed doing odd things? No, as anyone who knew him would deny. Grenfell was simply a young Christian ready to serve—and that is all it takes for a whole country to rise in hope.

A little background: One night in London, while coming home from a sick call, Grenfell slipped into a tent where Dwight Moody, a famous American evangelist, was holding meetings. Grenfell sat down on a back bench. A fellow preacher was offering the prayer before the sermon—a very long prayer. Thinking he had more important work to do, Grenfell quietly rose to leave.

But Moody, catching on to what was happening, quickly rose to his feet also and boomed out to the audience, "Let us sing a hymn while our brother finishes his prayer!"

In his autobiography Grenfell wrote that any man who had that much common sense was worth listening to. Then he penned, "When I left that meeting, it was with the determination to make religion a real effort, to do as I thought Christ would do in my place as a doctor, or frankly abandon it."

Forty years later Grenfell looked back on the fruit of this determination and wrote: "I see more clearly that the value of a man's religion must be measured by what it has enabled him to do."

And do he did. Before Grenfell died he had founded an association to care for six hospitals, seven nursing stations, four hospital ships, four agricultural stations, 12 clothing distribution centers, a seaman's institute, a supply schooner, a cooperative lumber mill, and a repair ship for fishing boats—besides the untold pain he removed, the lives he prolonged, and the Christian hope he revived.

Dr. Grenfell understood Paul, and he listened closely to the call of Jesus.

But Paul wants to make sure that his readers understand that the Christian life is not merely a quiet assent to God—that all Christians have to do is believe what the Bible says about Jesus being our Saviour. After all his penetrating theological instruction and keen description of the Christian life in Colossians 3, Paul emphasizes again that the bottom line of the Christian's response to God's grace is a matter of thinking and doing the Lord's business (verse 23). The test of whether the Christian has caught on to his privileges is whether he goes forth with *enthusiasm* ("heartily" can be a literal translation; "from the soul"—not superficially, especially when others are watching!). What common sense, especially after one understands the principles of the great controversy!

What drives people on, whatever the task? What keeps people keeping on when circumstances seem so forbidding? Paul said you may know "that from the Lord you will receive the inheritance as your reward; you are serving the Lord Christ" (verse 24). The word is called hope (see chapter 7). Hope is the most compelling motivator in the universe, regardless of what or in whom a person may hope. But for us who hope in "the inheritance as [our] reward," eternal fellowship with Jesus, after giving Him our highest and best service, is truly the most powerful engine that could pull us into the future.

Think of Polycarp, bishop of old Smyrna (modern Izmir) in western Turkey, who lived approximately between A.D. 70-160. Irenaeus, another early church father, heard Polycarp speak of his conversations with John the apostle and other eyewitnesses of Jesus.

He retired for the night, knowing that the Roman soldiers were nearby and looking for him; yet, he could sleep even though he knew that his hours were numbered.

Awakened by clanging metal in the street and the loud knock of the legionnaire, the veteran Christian leader invited the soldiers in, called for his household, and served refreshments. Then with the same serenity, fully realizing that his end was at hand, he made one last request—only one quiet hour to spend with his Lord.

One hour later Polycarp was led to the proconsul. The crowd gathered, some to watch the torture and death, others to beg the man they respected to renounce his faith in Christ: "Simply say 'Lord Caesar.'"

Philip, the proconsul, urged, "Only swear by Caesar and reproach this Christ."

But he replied, "Eighty and six years have I served Him, and He never did me wrong. How can I blaspheme the King that hath saved me?"

Angered, Philip threatened, "I have wild beasts at hand; I will cast you to these unless you change your mind."

"Call them," Polycarp replied, "for we have no reason to repent from the better to the worse, but it is good to change from wickedness to virtue."

Fully frustrated with the friend he was trying to save, Philip finally said, "I will cause you to be consumed by fire should you not change your mind."

Polycarp calmly responded, "You threaten fire that burns for the moment, for you know nothing of the judgment to come and the punishment reserved for the wicked."

So Polycarp was led to the stake. He was not bound, as was the custom, but stood in the midst of the flames, eyes fixed on heaven, lips moving in prayer, until the end came and his tortured body rested.

There have been many Polycarps in this world. Not always was it the fiery stake, or the garrote, or the cross, or the sword, or the machine gun, or the gas chamber. It may have been a defeated kidney, a worn-out heart, or a breast devastated before its time. Whatever, these Polycarps died with hope, in peace, "knowing that from the Lord [they] will receive the inheritance."

The Christian's hope makes a difference. True, for Christians as well as for their friends, the simple fact becomes clearer the longer one lives: life is a series of partings all welded together with sorrow. But for the Christian, the goodbye is not forever; though wrapped in sadness, it is not despair. The goodbye is a shout of hope!

Paul wrote elsewhere that "in the twinkling of an eye . . . we shall be changed" (1 Cor. 15:52).

Oh, how we need to be changed! We speak not of our personalities and character weaknesses—all this will have to be changed before the resurrection (see chapter 6). But we speak of these tired bodies, the sinus or migraine headaches, the weakened heart, that sciatic nerve, the creeping cancer, the fatigue that comes before our day's work is done. All this will be gone when the heavens part and the angel sounds the trumpet, when the heavenly paratroopers wing families together from all parts of the world.

Somebody's sweetheart, somebody's father or mother, somebody's son or daughter, brother, husband, or wife, lies at the bottom of every ocean, under the soil of a thousand battlefields, beneath millions of headstones. But in the twinkling of an eye all this will be changed. Thousands, yes, millions, whole and alive, laughing and hugging—all thrilled beyond words. Warm hands, moist lips, the familiar hug, and the smile—all restored.

This is the smashing victory of "our Lord Jesus Christ" (verse 57), the glorious good news of the resurrection morning just ahead—"the inheritance." Isn't that a great reason for joy? Believe it!

Capturing Joy in Service

15

"The law of love calls for the devotion of body, mind, and soul to the service of God and our fellowmen. And this service, while making us a blessing to others, brings the greatest blessing to ourselves. Unselfishness underlies all true development. Through unselfish service we receive the highest culture of every faculty. More and more fully do we become partakers of the divine nature. We are fitted for heaven, for we receive heaven into our hearts" *(Education,* p. 16).

THIS book is about joy and the rock foundations on which joy is built. It doesn't take much observation before we sense the question What's happened to joy? Is joy something that children and the naive can experience but not those who are supposed to know what's going on? Does a realistic appraisal of life require a gloomy disposition?

Why is it that many religious people rarely smile? What is there about their theology that makes them abrasive, crabby, and cheerless? Surely there is something missing in a person's religion if joy is gone.

Furthermore, a joyless religion and disposition is not strictly a personal matter any more than cigarette smoking is. Gloom is a noxious fog that demoralizes everyone within shouting distance. Pontifical highhandedness seems to be associated with the lack of joy. Another is social intimidation, whereby everyone is forced to "walk on eggs" to avoid the scowl or worse from the joyless member.

What about Jesus? Does He come through with a frown—a

glum yet determined crusader for righteousness? Hardly! Not *that* Man who attracted young people to Him wherever He went. Children do not climb all over a grump! Besides, a Man who had a social circle that included town mayors, university teachers, fishermen, internal revenue agents, and ex-prostitutes could not have been a killjoy. He added to every group; He didn't subtract.

Gloom, remorse, self-depreciation—such are not signs of humility, certainly not Christlikeness. More likely a sour face is evidence of poor or selective theology and a deficient picture of God. My favorite author said it right: "The Christian's life should be one of faith, of victory, and joy in God" (*The Great Controversy*, p. 477).

Whenever early Christians truly preached the truth about Jesus, "there was much joy in that city" (Acts 8:8). For Paul, joy was one evidence that a person was led by the Holy Spirit (Gal. 5:22).

However, preaching the gospel does not necessarily produce joy. Although the facts may be correct, the emphasis and tone of the speaker may not reflect joy. Notice this helpful counsel:

"The world [has] received the idea from the attitude of the church that God's people are indeed a joyless people, that the service of Christ is unattractive, that the blessing of God is bestowed at severe cost to the receivers. By dwelling upon our trials, and making much of difficulties, we misrepresent God and Jesus Christ whom He has sent; for the path to heaven is made unattractive by the gloom that gathers about the soul of the believer, and many turn in disappointment from the service of Christ" (*Testimonies to Ministers*, p. 175).

Only joy produces joy! That is why Paul's writings have met the test of time and of experience—joy is the golden thread throughout his letters. That's why he could make a chapel out of a prison; that's why prison walls did not shut down the possibility of preaching again. He had joy beyond belief, and joy cannot be cooped up! It has to be shared.

Paul learned well his Master's secret. He learned quickly that his Master knew that the main thing was to keep the main thing the main thing! The main thing: the river of joy must be shared, or it soon becomes a swamp of gloom. Our Lord's main thing was "that my joy may be in you, and that your joy may be full" (John 15:11).

Listen to Paul's request to his Colossian friends: "Pray for us . . . that God may open to us a door for the word, to declare the mystery of Christ" (Col. 4:3). Of course, Paul wanted to get out of prison, but not primarily to escape suffering. He wanted a door of opportunity open once more so that he could preach the good news again, the "mystery, which is Christ in you, the hope of glory" (Col. 1:27).

The old fire horse wanted to hear the bell just once more! Every true preacher should be like that until the day he dies. The measure of our Christian commitment is easily taken by the joy we have for service, for the next opportunity to bring Jesus to someone who has never really been introduced to Him personally.

And he made another request. Strange, coming from the master preacher! But he wanted their prayers so that he may be even more clear, more convincing, more persuasive in his soul-winning ventures.

What a lesson for all Christians—we have never given the good news as clearly as we yet can make it! We still need divine help in knowing what we "ought to speak," no matter how "successful" we may have been in the past.

The Greek philosopher Heracleitus (540-480 B.C.) is reported to have said, "One cannot step into the same river twice." Remarkable concept. But never truer for an alert preacher. Every person, every audience, is different from the last. Every sermon, every approach, needs to be updated for the next opportunity.

Here is a man described by my favorite author as one who possessed "high intellectual endowments. . . . He had that greatest of all wisdom, which gives quickness of insight and sympathy of heart, which brings man in touch with men, and enables him to arouse their better nature and inspire them to a higher life. . . . See Paul at Athens before the council of the Areopagus, as he meets science with science, logic with logic, and philosophy with philosophy. Mark how, with the tact born of divine love, he points to Jehovah as the 'Unknown God.'. . . In service he found his joy" (*Education*, pp. 66-68).

Thus, the sign of greatest commitment and humility in soul

winners is their continual study of how to speak clearly, how to phrase their words to get fair, favorable, and undivided attention from their audience. But also, how to respond to every query—"how [we] ought to answer every one." Every new opportunity to say a word for Jesus requires a clear head in a healthy body, a willingness to put aside personal plans as well as Christian desire.

I think of Boris Kornfield, a Jewish Russian physician during the noonday of Communism in the land once called the Soviet Union. Jewish people were very active in behalf of the Russian Revolution in 1917. Some Jews became the Bolsheviks' strongest leaders. Many people have wondered why. Most of the Jews fell in with Communism for a very simple reason: for more than 200 years they had been terribly persecuted by the dominant Christian church throughout the great land of Russia, under the blessing of the czar.

One of the top officials in the Russian Orthodox Church once said, "We need to kill one third of the Jews, imprison another one third, and see that the other one third leave the country." You can see why Communism would appear as salvation to the Jew, in the light of that attitude.

But somehow Boris Kornfield got at cross-purposes with Stalin's secret agents and was sentenced to one of the gulags—those incredibly inhumane prison camps in Siberia. But he was a physician. In a prison camp the physician cared for everyone—the commander and the guards as well as the prisoners. Of course, physicians were treated with deference in comparison with other prisoners. After all, would you want to go under the surgeon's knife if the surgeon were someone who hated you and might let the knife slip? So Boris enjoyed some favors other prisoners never saw.

One day Kornfield talked with another prisoner, a patient. The patient quietly said he was a Christian, that he believed in the Bible, that he believed in God's Messiah, and that God's Messiah was a suffering Jew.

Sensing that Kornfield was still listening, the prisoner talked on. He talked of his prison sufferings as nothing to compare with the sufferings of the Messiah. Boris listened, with all the intense hatred he had for all Christians and for all that Christians had done to Jews through the years in the name of their Jesus Messiah.

Yet Kornfield saw in this man a calm confidence and conviction he had never seen before. Very quietly, very secretly, Kornfield accepted this Christ, this Messiah, as his Lord. He began a practice of reciting the Lord's Prayer during his surgeries and while doing his rounds.

Then he began to think about all the implications of this kind of commitment. He began to examine his own life. For example, it was routine that before any prisoner could be put into solitary confinement a doctor had to sign a document that said the prisoner was in good physical shape—which was nearly always a lie. Most men died in solitary confinement—and he had signed hundreds of such forms.

But now Kornfield decided that as a Christian he would no longer sign such forms—although he knew this refusal was tantamount to signing his own death warrant.

A few days passed. Every day in the hospital ward he had seen men dying of diseases that food could quickly heal. But on this particular day, after watching one more prisoner die unnecessarily, he saw an orderly, a turncoat prisoner, eating the bread that had been intended for the patients. Kornfield did what his new faith told him to do—he reported the orderly to the commandant.

The commandant was amused. "All right," he said, "we'll put the orderly into solitary confinement for three days." Kornfield knew that from that time on he was as good as dead.

A few days later, as Kornfield walked into his hospital's recovery room, he saw a patient who had just been operated on for cancer. Kornfield was used to seeing sorrow in faces, but a sadness and a depth of sensitivity was etched into this stranger's face that he had seen in no other prisoner. He immediately felt a strange bond with this patient.

And so Kornfield sat beside him and poured out what had happened in his life—that he was a Jew, that he had been disillusioned with Communism, that he had embraced God's Messiah, that he could no longer sign the solitary-confinement warrants— and that he knew he had only a very short time to live.

But he said, "I feel freer than any man in the Soviet Union, and I feel a joy I never knew existed."

The patient was drowsy from the anesthetic of his surgery, but he was so fascinated with Kornfield's comments that he held on to every word—and somehow stayed awake.

Later that night the patient listened for Kornfield to return as he had promised. He waited throughout the next morning. But his physician never returned. After Kornfield had left that patient to whom he had poured out his newly discovered faith in Jesus Christ, he had been struck in the head eight times—24 hours later he was dead.

But the patient Kornfield had talked to was Aleksandr Solzhenitsyn. He is probably Russia's greatest author of the twentieth century and one of the most profound speakers whom English-speaking people can listen to today. Long before Mikhail Gorbachev came to power, millions of people had learned about the gulags in Siberia through smuggled books written by Solzhenitsyn—especially the three volumes entitled *The Gulag Archipelago.*

The story is not over. Kornfield's determination to make the gospel clear, to make the most of his time on earth, and to know how he ought to answer every person (see Col. 4:4-6) got Solzhenitsyn to thinking about his own life. He was in prison because he too was at cross-purposes with Communism. But Christianity had never seemed a serious option—until Boris Kornfield came into his life.

But life in the gulag was so depressing, so suffocating. For long periods of time, the prisoners were not allowed to read or write, or even to speak. Then came the man who drew the cross in the sand—and Solzhenitsyn was never again the same. (Remember the story in chapter 8?)

Now my point: Who was that prisoner who dared to speak to Kornfield about his faith in Jesus Christ? What kind of power transformed Kornfield from a Christ-hater to His disciple, knowing that such a commitment would seal his death warrant? Who was that prisoner who drew the cross in the sand at the risk of his own life?

We don't know their names—but we do know that they are remembered in the Lamb's book of life! They, along with thousands of faithful witnesses through the centuries, prayed that they would "know how [they] ought to answer every one" (verse 6).

Some time in the near future we all will have the opportunity to speak for Jesus, and maybe—just maybe—we will be risking everything we own or desire. Are we, like Paul, praying that we will be able "to make it clear, as [we] ought to speak," making the most of the time, "that we may know how [we] ought to answer every one"?

Paul has more to say about how we may make those doors of opportunity truly effective. "Conduct yourselves wisely toward outsiders" (verse 5).

"Outsiders"—a term that some people think that Adventists made up! It really is a tender term—"outsiders" are our Lord's children, as well as those "inside." What if we were on the outside today? What difference would it make in our lives? Surely it would be a dreary walk in this crazy world. What are the happy reasons that you are glad you now know, since you have been on the "inside"? What are your reasons for joy? That's a lot to talk about with "outsiders"!

But how do we relate to outsiders? It takes more than a Bible in the hand. Paul makes it clear that what outsiders see is even more important than what they hear. Listen to the following straightforward words to church members who sense they are special people with a special message for a special time:

"Character is power. The silent witness of a true, unselfish, godly life carries an almost irresistible influence. By revealing in our own life the character of Christ we cooperate with Him in the work of saving souls. It is only by revealing in our life His character that we can cooperate with Him. And the wider the sphere of our influence, the more good we may do. When those who profess to serve God follow Christ's example, practicing the principles of the law in their daily life; when every act bears witness that they love God supremely and their neighbor as themselves, then will the church have power to move the world" (*Christ's Object Lessons*, p. 340).

That word for "time" (Col. 4:5)—we need to pause here for a moment. The Greeks had five words translated "time" in English. The Greek word Paul uses in verse 5 is *kairos*, which implies a specialness, a quality moment, an opportunity or fulfillment such as when used in referring to our Lord's first and second coming (for some examples: Matt. 13:30; 16:3; 21:34; 26:18; Mark 13:33; Luke 19:44; 21:8; John 7:6; Rom. 5:6; Eph. 1:10; Rev. 1:3).

The other most often used Greek word that we translate "time" is *chronos,* or measured time (as minutes, hours, years, etc.). When we say "It is now 7:00 p.m." (as it is for me at this moment), we are using *chronos* time.

When we quote 2 Corinthians 6:2—"Now is the accepted time; behold, now is the day of salvation"—we are using *kairos* time. Opportunity, fulfillment, specialness—all wrapped up in *kairos*, the word Paul uses here in Colossians 4:5. Any time we have a window of opportunity open to say a clear word about Jesus Christ—that is a special moment, an opportune time. Seize the time, the *kairos!*

(A valuable distinction between *chronos* and *kairos* in reference to the time in which we now live, the *kairos* of Adventist opportunity and responsibility, will be found in Jack Provonsha's *A Remnant in Crisis* [Hagerstown, Md.: Review and Herald Pub. Assn., 1993], pp. 123-136.)

Paul is not finished. He is so thorough, so pastoral! One of the ways we prepare for those moments of *kairos* is to improve our speech patterns, especially if we intend to speak in public (Col. 4:6). Two special qualities that we are not born with—"gracious" and "seasoned"—are the Christian's greatest tools for making the good news attractive.

No, we are not suggesting contrived oiliness, or even the pleasantries of a diplomat. Remember, early in His ministry our Lord came to the synagogue at Nazareth on the Sabbath. He was asked to read the scripture and give the message. The response of the people suggests that Jesus had learned how to speak graciously, seasoning His words with "salt." "And all spoke well of him, and wondered at the gracious words which proceeded out of his mouth; and they said, 'Is not this Joseph's son?'" (Luke 4:22).

Mary and Joseph trained Jesus well. So should we help our children today: "The chief requisite of language is that it be pure and kind and true—'the outward expression of an inward grace.'. . . The best school for this language study is the home.

"Kind words are as dew and gentle showers to the soul. The Scripture says of Christ that grace was poured into His lips, that He might 'know how to speak a word in season to him that is weary.' And the Lord bids us, 'Let your speech be alway with grace,' 'that it may minister grace unto the hearers'" (*The Adventist Home*, p. 435).

What could Paul mean by "seasoned with salt"? When my wife seasons our food, I get the idea that she uses not too much and not too little of what she wants to enhance our food with. Although we go very easy with salt, we know when we need it!

In Paul's day salt was the preserver of food—but it had to be carefully done. Our speech, carefully preserved from blandness as well as demoralizing chatter, should make our message attractive, not insipid. This takes practice! We won't be ready for our special *kairos*—that is, our window of opportunity to witness—if we are not building good habits of speech during the *chronos* of our lives.

The rest of Colossians 4 tells us much about Paul. He was not a one-man show; he was a team player. It must have been the greatest experience that any Christian minister could have had in the past 1,900 years to have interned under Paul.

He knew how to affirm self-worth, how to encourage and assist in handling big projects. Follow his public expressions of confidence for his colleagues—Tychicus, Onesimus, Aristarchus, Mark, Justus, Epaphras, Luke (oh, what a pal this physician was), Demas (before his apostasy), Nympha, and Archippus. Men and women, young and old alike! What a leader!

I was fortunate to intern under a prince of the church—he was everything to me that Paul was to Timothy. That man went on to become president of the Florida Conference. He was loved and respected so much that he was elected president of the Southern Union, where he served for many years. I can understand Paul better because of Schmitty! He and Doris are all joy! I trust that I have passed on what I learned from them.

Philippians and Colossians—on one hand they are like strong, steel-girded buildings. On the other, they are sky-high poems, singing out the joy of Christianity, even under the toughest of times.

If you have stuck by this book this far, I hope you have been infected with Christian joy. Without joy, my life would have lost all meaning years ago. It has made all the difference.